25 YEARS

LOTUS SEVEN

Collection No.1

Compiled by
R.M. Clarke

ISBN 0 907 073 506

Distributed by
Brooklands Book Distribution Ltd.
'Holmerise', Seven Hills Road,
Cobham, Surrey, England

Brooklands Books Titles in this series

AC Cobra 1962-1969
Armstrong Siddeley Cars 1945-1960
Austin 7 in the Thirties
Austin Seven Cars 1930-1935
Austin 10 1932-1939
Austin Healey 100 1952-1959
Austin Healey 3000 1959-1967
Austin Healey 100 & 3000 Collection No. 1
Austin Healey Sprite 1958-1971
Bentley Cars 1919-1929
Bentley Cars 1929-1934
Bentley Cars 1934-1939
Bentley Cars 1940-1945
Bentley Cars 1945-1950
BMW 1600 Collection No. 1
BMW 2002 Collection No. 1
Buick Cars 1929-1939
Camaro 1966-1970
Chrysler Cars 1930-1939
Citroen Traction Avant 1934-1957
Citroen 2CV 1949-1982
Corvette Cars 1955-1964
Datsun 240z & 260z 1970-1977
De Tomaso Collection No. 1
Dodge Cars 1924-1938
Ferrari Cars 1946-1956
Ferrari Cars 1957-1962
Ferrari Cars 1962-1966
Ferrari Cars 1966-1969
Ferrari Cars 1969-1973
Ferrari Cars 1973-1977
Ferrari Cars 1977-1981
Ferrari Collection No. 1
Fiat X1/9 1972-1980
Ford GT40 1964-1978
Ford Mustang 1964-1967
Ford Mustang 1967-1973
Ford RS Escort 1968-1980
Hudson & Railton Cars 1936-1940
Jaguar (& S.S) Cars 1931-1937
Jaguar (& S.S) Cars 1937-1947
Jaguar Cars 1948-1951
Jaguar Cars 1951-1953
Jaguar Cars 1954-1955
Jaguar Cars 1955-1957
Jaguar Cars 1957-1961
Jaguar Cars 1961-1964
Jaguar Cars 1964-1968
Jaguar Sports Cars 1957-1960
Jaguar E-Type 1961-1966
Jaguar E-Type 1966-1971
Jaguar E-Type 1971-1975
Jaguar XKE Collection No. 1
Jaguar XJ6 1968-1972
Jaguar XJ6 1973-1980
Jaguar XJ12 1972-1980
Jaguar XJS 1975-1980
Jensen Cars 1946-1967
Jensen Cars 1967-1979
Jensen Interceptor 1966-1976
Jensen-Healey 1972-1976
Lamborghini Cars 1964-1970
Lamborghini Cars 1970-1975
Land Rover 1948-1973
Lotus Elan 1962-1973
Lotus Elan Collection No. 1
Lotus Elite & Eclat 1975-1981
Lotus Esprit 1974-1981
Lotus Europa 1966-1975
Lotus Europa Collection No. 1
Lotus Seven 1957-1980
Lotus Seven Collection No. 1
Maserati 1965-1970
Maserati 1970-1975
Mazda RX-7 Collection No. 1
Mercedes Benz Cars 1949-1954
Mercedes Benz Cars 1954-1957
Mercedes Benz Cars 1957-1961
Mercedes Benz Competition Cars 1950-1957
MG Cars in the Thirties
MG Cars 1929-1934
MG Cars 1935-1940
MG Cars 1940-1947
MG Cars 1948-1951
MG Cars 1952-1954
MG Cars 1955-1957
MG Cars 1957-1959
MG Cars 1959-1962
MG Midget 1961-1979
MG MGA 1955-1962
MG MGB 1962-1970
MG MGB 1970-1980
MG MGB GT 1965-1980
Mini-Cooper 1961-1971
Morgan 3-Wheeler 1930-1952
Morgan Cars 1936-1960
Morgan Cars 1960-1970
Morgan Cars 1969-1979
Morris Minor 1949-1970
Morris Minor Collection No. 1
Nash Metropolitan 1954-1961
Packard Cars 1920-1942
Pantera 1970-1973
Pantera & Mangusta 1969-1974
Pontiac GTO 1964-1970
Pontiac Firebird 1967-1973
Porsche Cars 1952-1956
Porsche Cars 1957-1960
Porsche Cars 1960-1964
Porsche Cars 1964-1968
Porsche Cars 1968-1972
Porsche Cars 1972-1975
Porsche Cars in the Sixties
Porsche 914 1969-1975
Porsche 911 Collection No. 1
Porsche 911 Collection No. 2
Porsche 924 1975-1981
Porsche 928 Collection No. 1
Porsche Turbo Collection No. 1
Riley Cars 1932-1935
Riley Cars 1936-1939
Riley Cars 1940-1945
Riley Cars 1945-1950
Riley Cars 1950-1955
Rolls Royce Cars 1930-1935
Rolls Royce Cars 1935-1940
Rolls Royce Cars 1940-1950
Rollys-Royce Silver Shadow 1965-1980
Range Rover 1970-1981
Rover P4 1949-1959
Rover P4 1955-1964
Singer Sports Cars 1933-1954
Studebaker Cars 1923-1939
Sunbeam Alpine & Tiger 1959-1967
Triumph Spitfire 1962-1980
Triumph Stag 1970-1980
Triumph TR2 & TR3 1952-1960
Triumph TR4 & TR5 1961-1969
Triumph GT6 1966-1974
TVR 1960-1980
Volkswagen Cars 1936-1956
VW Beetle 1956-1977
VW Karmann Ghia Collection No. 1
Volvo 1800 1960-1973
Volvo 120 Series 1956-1970

CONTENTS

ACKNOWLEDGEMENTS

It is a very enjoyable task to research a book on the Lotus Seven and doubly so when it is to celebrate its 25th year in production. Jonathan Wood in his book British Post War Classics described it as 'a basic two-seater with outstanding road holding but with weather equipment that was not for the fainthearted!' As one who was driving a Morgan 3-Wheeler Super Sports which was 25 years old when the Seven was born, I well know the sensations.

For owners who would like further information on this race proven vehicle a completely different set of articles trace the Seven story from its inception in a companion volume Lotus Seven 1957-1980.

The Brooklands Books series perhaps more than any other publications rely on the help and goodwill of numerous people and companies who understand the value to enthusiasts of a reference work such as this. Our thanks go firstly to the management of the journals who have allowed their copyright articles to be included here – Asian Auto, Autocar, Autosport, Car, Motor, Motor Sport, Road & Track, Sports Cars Illustrated, Sports Car & Lotus Owner and Sports Car World. Secondly our thanks go to Graham Nearn and David Wakefield of Caterham Cars who supplied the attractive cover photograph and who offered support when it was most needed and lastly to Ray Girling of Chelmsford who kindly supplied pictures of his 'Jubilee' Super Seven which can be seen on page 70. My ambition now is to be around for the celebration of the Sevens fiftieth anniversary.

R.M. Clarke

Reasonable protection is provided by the lightweight hood, which is easy to erect. The cutaway body sides allow plenty of elbow room. The radiator cowling is quickly detachable

Autocar ROAD TESTS 1664

Lotus Seven

SPORTS cars today, apart from classes which have engine capacity as the main basis of classification, may be divided into three categories. There are the expensive continental hand-built models; there is a hard core of two-seaters made—mostly in Great Britain—in quantity by long-established manufacturers; and the remainder are the individually built sports cars of small manufacturers, from whose ranks come many entries for club race meetings in this country.

Many of the last-named have chassis of tubular ladder or space frame construction, and they use a variety of proprietary engines and transmissions. The Lotus comes under this heading, and the current aerodynamic models of 1½ litres and 1,100 c.c. have been outstandingly successful in international racing. Until last October the cheapest Lotus in production was the 1,172 c.c. club model which with purchase tax costs £1,511.

The model which established the reputation of Lotus was the Mark VI, as it was a very popular jumping-off point for the young enthusiast who wished to enter sports car racing without too much expenditure, and it could be used also as a normal road car, albeit with some degree of discomfort. It is two years since this model was produced, and the second-hand value has remained at a remarkably high figure.

To fill the gap caused by the discontinuance of this model, Lotus Engineering announced the Lotus Seven at the last Earls Court Show. Its object is the same as that of its predecessor, but it has a more up-to-date specification. When fitted with the four-cylinder side-valve Ford engine, it qualifies for the 1,172 c.c. formula in popular club events. The price with purchase tax of the basic model is £1,036; additional fittings are twin carburettors, special exhaust, hood and tonneau cover.

It is possible, however, to purchase frame, engine, gear box and other parts separately. If they are assembled by the purchaser with no professional help or facilities, purchase tax is not payable and the price is £526. The simple style of body of the Lotus Seven naturally helps to lower cost, as compared with the aerodynamic design of the other models.

The chassis frame of tubular construction is very similar to that of the more expensive streamlined models, and the front suspension is like that of the formula 2, with wishbones and coil springs. At the rear, a normal live axle is suspended on coil springs and located by radius arms. The body has no doors, but the cockpit sides are lowered so that they are easy to step over; entrance is a little more difficult with the hood erected. Without doors, the car cannot be used for International races, but it is not excluded from club meetings in this country. The front wheels are exposed, with separate

***Left:** With a height of 2ft 3½in to the top of the scuttle the Lotus Seven is a dwarf among other traffic. **Right:** The spare wheel rests in a tubular bracket and is secured by a leather strap. Brake stop lights and reflectors are incorporated in the rear lamps*

Under-bonnet accessibility is not handicapped by the equipment usually seen in a road test illustration. The electric S.U. fuel pump is mounted close to the bulkhead, and plastic pipes are used for the fuel lines. The front mudguards are quickly detachable

mud deflectors, and they can be clearly seen when placing the car for a fast corner.

The car tested has a Ford Prefect engine, gear box (fitted with Buckler C-type gears to improve the ratio steps) and rear axle. The compression ratio is raised to 8.5 to 1, and twin S.U. carburettors and special exhaust manifold were fitted. There is available a wide choice of axle ratios, ranging from 3.73 to 1 to 5.375 to 1. The test car had 4.875 to 1 ratio.

An outstanding feature of the car is the road-holding and general stability. The suspension is, by normal saloon car standards, stiff, but not to the degree of the sports car of twenty years ago. The coil springs used to support the car at front and rear enclose piston-type dampers. At the front there is an anti-roll bar, which serves also as an arm of the upper wishbone.

Speed on corners seems to be limited only by visibility and/or the driver's experience. At first the Lotus gives the impression of wandering and lacking directional stability, but this disappears as soon as the steering wheel is allowed to float in the driver's hands. "Hands off," the car will maintain a straight course. The steering is sensitive but free from any vice, and there are no noticeable over or understeer characteristics.

Although the steering has only two turns from lock to lock, the effort at the wheel is very low; one can take quick corrective action if the back end should hop, which it tends to do on bumpy corners, probably because of the relatively high proportion of unsprung weight in such a light car. There is no reaction from the front wheels and in this respect the new wishbone suspension is a great improvement on the swing axle type of the Mark VI, which was subject to gyroscopic kick and tended to wander on the straight.

No seat adjustment is provided, and the car tested suited a driver with long legs better than a short person; such a car would normally have the driving position tailored to its usual occupant. The small two-spoked steering wheel is almost vertical and close to the facia; the outstretched position of the driver's arms is comfortable and gives full control. Cockpit space is limited and there is not much foot room around the pedals, though their angles are excellent and comfortable. Brake pedal and accelerator are set so that "heel and toe" changes become a natural manœuvre. The handbrake lever, which has horizontal movement, pivots on the passenger's side of the cockpit; it is difficult to reach when needed for restarting on a steep hill.

When driving the Lotus Seven in reasonably traffic-free conditions one soon forgets minor discomforts in the exhilaration of its performance, and the manner of its achievement. The Prefect engine, mildly tuned in this case, gives an excellent power-weight ratio and, except for some reluctance to start when really cold, has no temperament.

The engine quickly reaches operating temperature (no fan or water pump is fitted) and it will then give full throttle response without hesitation. The exhaust note at high engine revolutions is noticeable, but the car can be driven quietly through built-up areas without attracting attention other than by its appearance. Acceleration in the open country is very good, and 35 m.p.h. on the high first gear is reached very quickly with a hard snarl from the exhaust. Second gear ratio is close enough to top to give valuable hill-climbing performance. It provides a maximum speed of 70 m.p.h. and is very useful for overtaking at speeds in excess of 50 m.p.h.

Some saloon cars with not much larger engines, and capable of carrying four or more persons in greater comfort, have higher maximum speeds than the Lotus, but their occupants may never know the joy of driving such a car. It is a great pity that purchase tax prevents such cars as this, with especially high safety factors of road-holding, from reaching the hands of so many young enthuiasts who would benefit by the experience.

The maximum speed of 81 m.p.h. with two aboard is creditable. With a small racing screen and further tuning of the engine, 90 m.p.h. should be possible solo.

The light weight of the Lotus makes a three-speed gear box acceptable. No reverse stop is provided, so that sometimes reverse gear is "snicked" when coming out of first. Very quick, definite changes can be made, but some care and practice is required to engage bottom when changing down from second. The clutch pedal pressure appeared fairly high—indicative of stronger springs than standard. No clutch slip occurred during repeated standing start acceleration tests, and take-off was smooth once the short, stiff travel of the pedal had been mastered.

The fuel tank, strapped down by aero-elastic bands in the extreme rear with the small battery alongside it, adds valuable extra weight over the rear wheels and helps to balance the weight distribution.

Brakes of a size normally fitted to larger and heavier cars are used on the Lotus. There are two-leading shoes in the front units, and the system is smooth and progressive.

These characteristics at first may not appear to be

Left: The handbrake lever moves in a horizontal plane on the left side of the compartment. The facia panel is fabric-covered to match the trim. Right: Tool kit and the jack are strapped in the luggage space. The fuel tank and battery can be reached by removing the plywood floor

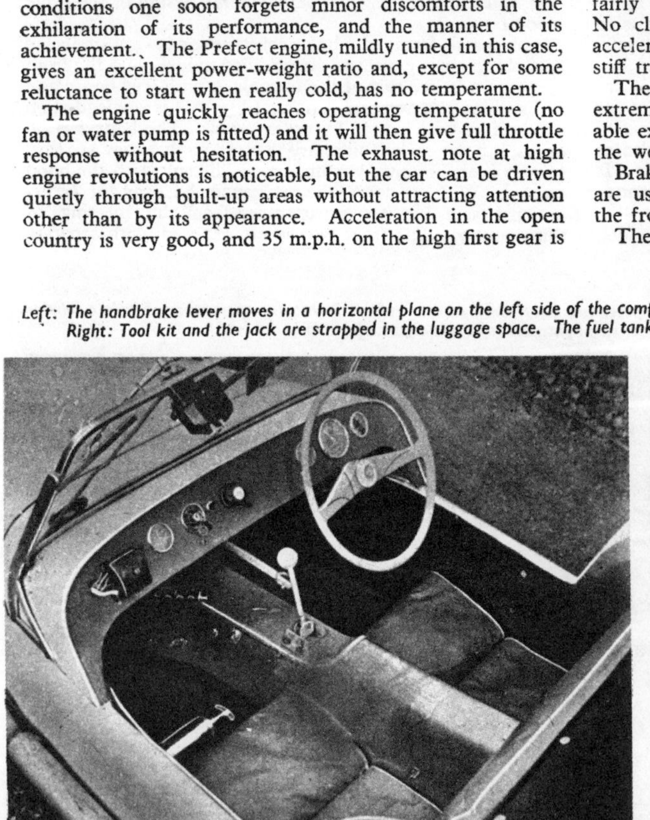

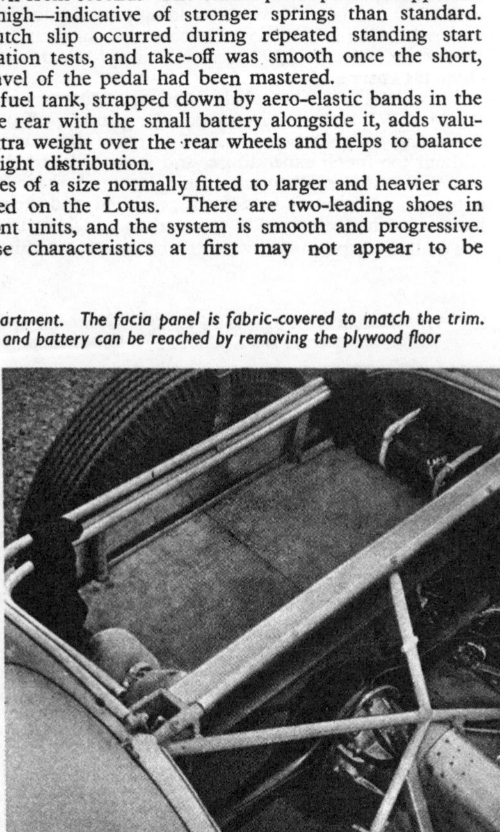

Lotus Seven . . .

reconciled with the performance figures quoted in the data tables. The reason for the seemingly low efficiency is that at pedal pressures above 50 lb sq in, with two occupants aboard, the front wheels tend to lock at the 30 m.p.h. testing speed, indicating that the braking ratio on the front wheels is too high at present. This could be adjusted by varying the sizes of operating cylinders or, more economically, by having the same size brakes at front and rear. It is a rare occurrence for this journal to comment that the brakes are too powerful, but on the Lotus care was needed in applying them on wet roads to avoid locking the front wheels and losing adhesion for steering.

The driving lamps—a wide beam unit on the left and a long-range lamp on the right—are quickly detachable; the wiring used for the head lamp circuit appears to be unusually light. A switch on the facia incorporating the horn button cuts out the right-hand lamp for dipping purposes. The full width windscreen frame is secured by four bolts and can be removed easily. Twin wipers are fitted; the wiper motor is prominent and could be a danger to a passenger.

A hood and tonneau cover can be had; the hood affords reasonable protection, although as no rain was experienced during the test it could not be fully checked. Normally it is housed, with the light alloy hood sticks, in a small compartment behind the cockpit. A good quality tool kit and hydraulic jack are strapped in this compartment. The facia panel is fitted with the required minimum number of instruments. There is no fuel gauge, but a graduated dip stick is provided.

The hydraulic brake fluid reservoir is reasonably easy to reach for topping up purposes.

For the enthusiast with a desire for racing the Lotus Seven is a safe and sensible vehicle. Purchase tax makes it expensive, but those who can build it up themselves can avoid this burden. In its dual form of racer and road car it is particularly suitable for the young beginner; with diligence he can improve the standards of comfort for road use without detracting from its racing performance.

LOTUS SEVEN

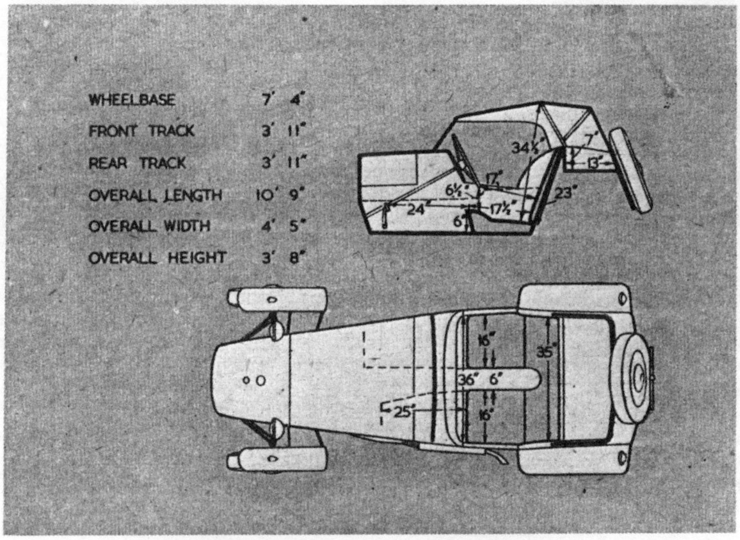

WHEELBASE 7' 4"
FRONT TRACK 3' 11"
REAR TRACK 3' 11"
OVERALL LENGTH 10' 9"
OVERALL WIDTH 4' 5"
OVERALL HEIGHT 3' 8"

Measurements in these ¼in to 1ft scale body diagrams are taken with the driving seat in the central position of fore and aft adjustment and with the seat cushions uncompressed

PERFORMANCE

ACCELERATION: from constant speeds.
Speed Range, Gear Ratios and Time in sec.

M.P.H.	4.875 to 1	6.483 to 1	11.407 to 1
10—30	—	6.5	3.5
20—40	7.6	6.2	—
30—50	7.9	7.1	—
40—60	10.1	9.3	—
50—70	16.5	—	—

From rest through gears to:

M.P.H.	sec
30	4.7
50	11.7
60	17.8
70	30.7

Standing quarter mile, 20.8 sec.

SPEEDS ON GEARS:

Gear		M.P.H. (normal and max.)	K.P.H. (normal and max.)
Top	(mean)	76.3	122.8
	(best)	81.0	130.4
2nd		55—70	88—112
1st		25—40	40—64

TRACTIVE RESISTANCE: 17.5 lb per ton at 10 M.P.H.

TRACTIVE EFFORT:

	Pull (lb per ton)	Equivalent Gradient
Top	215	1 in 10.4
Second	310	1 in 7.1

BRAKES (in neutral at 30 m.p.h.)

Efficiency	Pedal Pressure (lb)
69 per cent	50
37 per cent	25
31 per cent	15

FUEL CONSUMPTION:
35.6 m.p.g. overall for 615 miles (7.9 litres per 100 km).
Approximate normal range 27–43 m.p.g. 10.4–6.5 litres per 100 km).
Fuel, premium grade.

WEATHER: Cloudy, slight head wind, dry.
Air temperature, 45–50 deg F.
Acceleration figures are the means of several runs in opposite directions.
Tractive effort and resistance obtained by Tapley meter.

DATA

PRICE (basic), with two-seater body, **£690.**
British purchase tax, **£346 7s.**
Total (in Great Britain), **£1,036 7s.**

ENGINE: Capacity: 1,172 c.c. (71.55 cu in).
Number of cylinders: 4.
Bore and stroke: 63.5 × 92.5 mm. (2.5 × 3.64in).
Valve gear: side valve.
Compression ratio: 8.5 to 1.
B.H.P.: 40 at 4,500 r.p.m. (B.H.P. per ton laden 65.9).
Torque: 58 lb ft at 2,600 r.p.m.
M.P.H. per 1,000 r.p.m. on top gear, 15.6.

WEIGHT: (with 5 gals fuel), 9 cwt (1,008 lb).
Weight distribution (per cent): F, 50; R, 50.
Laden as tested: 12 cwt (1,358 lb).
Lb per c.c. (laden): 1.2.

BRAKES: Type: Girling. 2 LS front, L and T rear.
Method of operation: hydraulic.
Drum dimensions: F, 9in diameter; 1¾in wide. R, 8in diameter; 1¼in wide.
Lining area: F, 61 sq in. R, 48 sq in (181 sq in per ton laden).

TYRES: 5.20—15in.
Pressures (lb sq in): F, 18; R, 22 (normal).

TANK CAPACITY: 7 Imperial gallons.
Oil sump, 4½ pints.
Cooling system, 12 pints.

TURNING CIRCLE: 32ft (L. and R).
Steering wheel turns (lock to lock): 2.

DIMENSIONS: Wheelbase: 7ft. 4in.
Track: F, 3ft 11in; R, 3ft 11in.
Length (overall): 10ft 9in.
Height: 2ft 3½in, to top of scuttle.
Width: 4ft 5in.
Ground clearance: 5in.
Frontal area: 10 sq ft (approximately).

ELECTRICAL SYSTEM: 12-volt; 34 ampére-hour battery.
Head lights: single dip; 36 watt bulbs.

SUSPENSION: Front, independent, coil springs and wishbones with anti-roll bar. Rear, coil springs, live axle with trailing links.

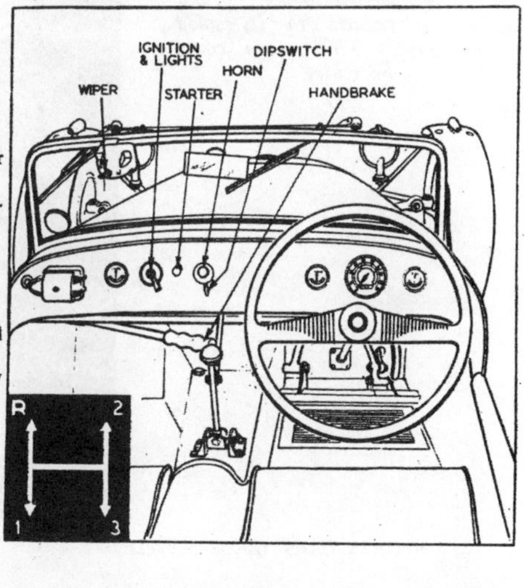

TOURING TRIAL No. 9

LOTUS SEVEN

Seen from above, the Lotus Seven is the starkest design available to-day. Yet everything about it is completely practical

UNDOUBTEDLY part of the Lotus legend or magic, is the fact that cynical motoring writers positively fight over the opportunity to subject a car of this make to a road test at the most unsuitable time of the year. During the spring and summer, when it would be sheer delight to drive any Lotus model, none are available, because the resources of the Lotus Engineering Co. Ltd., are stretched to the limit making and preparing cars for the ever growing number of people who want to go racing in Lotus cars. In the winter months however, almost every member of the staff of every motoring journal enjoys the opportunity of getting soaked to the skin.

The word "enjoys" is used advisedly, however, because there is no doubt that for sheer pleasure, a Lotus is very hard to beat. This is particularly true of the Seven, which is intended for sporting motoring rather than competition, although there is no doubt that as this model becomes more readily available it will become as familiar a feature in club events all over this country as the Elevens are in International meetings, and probably just as successful.

Introduced at Motor Show time last year, the Seven is an interesting design. It offers the enthusiastic motorist the opportunity of buying at a comparatively reasonable price, an exceptionally lively, out-and-out sports car with none of the complication and expense involved in a car designed for the ultimate in high performance. Thus it uses basically the same frame and front suspension as the Le Mans winning Eleven, but in place of the costly overhead camshaft engine, four-speed gearbox, de Dion rear end, disc brakes and fully aerodynamic bodywork, it uses simpler, and hence less expensive items.

For example, the frame is a familiar Lotus multi-tubular structure comprising square and round steel tubes with the floor and propeller shaft tunnel forming part of the stressed whole. The frame is lighter than that of the Eleven because it does not have to carry the all-developing low drag body-

Without a background to give it scale, the Seven looks normal enough—a tribute to its good proportions. The screen could be wider

work, but its kinship with the frame of the Eleven is obvious. The front suspension consists of tubular lower wishbones and a forged upper arm triangulated with an anti-roll bar. Coil springs and telescopic shock absorbers are the suspension medium front and rear. At the rear a live axle is used controlled by a pair of parallel trailing arms at each side, and a Panhard rod. People new to the car are inclined to suggest that the springing is very hard, in the true vintage sports car fashion, but one can quickly demonstrate that in fact the springs are comparatively soft, while the shock absorbers are very firm. Thus the ride is surprisingly comfortable, leaving the driver and passenger untired even after journeying over rough roads; while the amount of roll is so small in cornering as to be almost undetectable.

Mounted almost completely rigidly in the frame is a Ford 100E engine of 1,172 c.c. capacity. The familiar Ford side valve four-cylinder unit can be obtained in various stages of tune, and as tested was equipped with two 1¼ in. S.U. carburetters, a compression ratio of 8.5 : 1, and a four-branch exhaust manifold leading into a single external silencer. Power output was reputed to be around 45 b.h.p. at 4,500 r.p.m., but the way the engine was able to run up to 6,000 r.p.m. without protest revealed that it had received some careful tuning. Nevertheless it idled smoothly, started readily and revealed no sign of temperament.

The normal Ford clutch is employed with a mechanical linkage, and is perfectly amenable to frequent stopping and starting in traffic, or to racing style gear changes. The only snag with the clutch concerns the pedal, which is somewhat cramped in the narrow end of the space frame, and it is necessary to operate it with the toe. A large man with wide shoes finds insufficient room for his left foot and care must be taken to insert the toe to ensure a clean disengagement.

The Ford three-speed gearbox is equipped with close ratio gears and a simple remote linkage. It is delightfully positive in operation and free from vices; it would however benefit by the addition of a stop to prevent accidental "snicking" of reverse gear when making a quick change from first to second. Every owner of a car with this gearbox will know all about this, which is made more likely in the Lotus because the short lever enables such quick, effortless changes to be made.

The rear axle is a B.M.C. unit, fitted as standard with a 4.875 : 1 final drive unit. Thus the emphasis is obviously on excellent acceleration, which as the test figures prove, is achieved without strain. The brakes are Girling hydraulic all round, the front drums being 9 in. in diameter and the shoes 1¾ in. wide, while at the rear the drums have a diameter of 8 in. and the linings are 1¼ in. wide. Very light pedal pressures produce all the retardation necessary, and in fact it was found that violent application of the pedal resulted in the front wheels locking. As the weight distribution of the Seven is almost exactly 50/50 front and rear, this was considered surprising, and the obvious solution seems to be the radical one of putting smaller brakes on the front wheels—perhaps the same size as at the back. The situation on the car tested was that Tapley efficiencies of around 80 per cent could be obtained with the lightest pressures, but care is needed on ice or wet conditions to prevent difficulties.

Steering, by Burman worm and nut, is typically Lotus; quick, responsive, and extremely accurate. Only two turns are required from lock to lock, and the Seven makes history as the first Lotus with a respectable turning circle—to wit, 31 ft. between kerbs. It must however be admitted, that on full lock in either direction, the wheels rub the stays supporting the cycle-type mudguards and the headlights.

Some controversy arose during the tests on the Lotus Seven concerning the road holding and the general comportment of the car on the road. A gentle hand on the steering wheel is certainly best, and the car can be controlled with so little effort that after a while one wonders whether thought control rather than muscles are steering it. It neither under-steers nor over-steers, but it can be put off its line into a corner by bumps in the surface. After a while one becomes so used to its responsiveness, that quite fantastic things can be attempted and the Seven never fails, even if the driver's courage comes near to failing towards the end. In other words, the Seven possesses more than ordinary road-holding qualities. One thing which was considered important, was that the amount of throttle opening really had a minimum influence on the way the car cornered; obviously it is better to take a corner with the throttle open but the car can be cornered equally safely on a trailing throttle.

Much of the time during which the Lotus was in our hands, the roads were either wet or icy. Yet it was found that the Seven could be driven safely at cruising speeds around the 60–65 m.p.h. mark with bursts to higher speeds when overtaking was necessary. On one run, during which very heavy traffic was encountered on the way back to London along A40, it was found that the time taken from Denham to Shepherd's Bush was a mere 15 minutes. On ice, all four wheels tended to "go" together, but application of power and/or steering correction resulted in control being regained immediately.

Certain types of road surface resulted in a peculiar weaving motion, which may have been due entirely to the combination of load and tyre pressures at the time. On the other hand, the relation of spring rates front and rear could be improved; this would result in a more steady ride over this particular type of road surface, and would probably

With the hood up (protection against vertical rain), the Lotus Seven is only 3 ft. 9 in. high overall; it is 10 ft. 3 in. long overall, and 4 ft. 5 in. wide. The track is 3 ft. 11 in., and the wheelbase 7 ft. 4 in. Ground clearance is 5 in.

eliminate the side-to-side weaving experienced. Yet another contributory factor may have been the fact that the wheels on this particular car had either never been balanced or were in need of re-balancing.

Despite all this, every journey in the Seven was exhilarating. There is no sound-proofing, of course, and only a minimum of protection against wind and weather. After a while the driver's right ear takes on the same rosy tint as the passenger's left, and similarly, if it is wet, as it was most of the time *S.C.I.* had it, then the driver's right elbow and the passenger's left, became more and more wet.

The exhaust note is hearty, and as the engine speed rises towards its peak, takes on a shrill note which is most stirring; coming up behind slower cars on the open road, it was found that by dropping down into second gear at speeds up to the 65 m.p.h. region produced enough noise to alert the driver of the car immediately ahead. As the car is only 3 ft. 9 in. high overall, and only 2 ft. 3 in. up to the scuttle, this was valuable, because drivers of large vehicles were frequently seen scrutinizing the mirror in an effort to discover what it was they could hear behind them, but not see. The horn is reasonably efficient, but the exhaust note is often more effective.

Top bonnet panel is easily removed for access to engine and the nose cowl is equally easily removed. The picture shows this model with twin S.U. carburetters and four-branch exhaust system

The nearness of the outside exhaust pipe to the driver, and the relatively small capacity of the silencer, made gear-changing a particular delight, even bottom gear being available without undue difficulty, because it was so easy to adjust road and engine speeds before engaging this unsynchronized ratio. One snag (literally) concerning gear-changing was the fact that the bolt attaching the lever to the control rod protruded on the driver's side, and took small lumps out of the knees of taller drivers.

Not even this, it must be confessed, reduced the pleasure of driving the car. Acceleration is so good that one uses it at the slightest provocation. From a standstill, 30 m.p.h. is reached in 4 sec., and 50 m.p.h. is seen on the combined speedometer/rev. counter in 9.8 sec. This time, recorded with two people in the car, is the average of four runs. In another 4 sec., 60 m.p.h. is reached, and then a quick change into top gear, and 70 m.p.h. is recorded in 26 sec., from a standing start. Acceleration (driver only aboard) in second and third gears was surprisingly well sustained, as these figures show:—

	2nd gear	*Top gear*
20–40	7.2	5.8
30–50	9.2	5.4
40–60	9.4	8.8
50–70	11.8	—

At no time was a completely dry road available for these figures, which are thus all the more remarkable. With a passenger accompanying the driver, acceleration was slower by 2–3 sec. At no time during the test was it possible to obtain a maximum speed reading. The highest corrected speed attained was 86 m.p.h., but the car was still accelerating hard, and it seemed likely that 90 m.p.h. should be well within its range. Even so, this was by no means a drawback, and the car was driven safely at far higher speeds than most other cars on the roads. The tractive efficiency of the Seven, with its extremely low centre of gravity, is exceptional; its stability generally is of a high order.

Maximum speed in first gear was 42 m.p.h.—equivalent to 6,000 r.p.m. according to the markings on the speedometer —while second, when conditions permitted, would reach 74 m.p.h. The low weight of the Seven—$9\frac{1}{4}$ cwt.—and the low axle ratio made it a real hill-climb car. In top gear, a gradient of 1 in 9 can be climbed without a change being necessary, while second will carry the car rapidly up 1 in 6.

With the 7 gallon fuel tank full, the Seven should be able to cover well over 200 miles; during our trials it averaged 28.4 m.p.g. Driving it quietly, with little use of the intermediate gears, over 40 m.p.g. should be possible.

Equipment is fairly comprehensive. There is a hood, but no side curtains, and the hood compartment is quite

There is ample leg room for an average adult in the Seven, but much of the available elbow room is external. The handbrake is particularly inconvenient in this model

capacious. It is sensibly lined with Polyeurothene, so that the tools do not rattle about. There is no fuel gauge, but a misleading dip-stick gives a rough indication of the quantity of fuel remaining in the tank. The lighting is not ideal for long journeys at night; the lamps are a Lucas wide beam and a narrow long-range unit respectively, but as they are almost on the same level as the driver's eyes, their efficiency is somewhat wasted. Moreover, the light from them reflects from the chromium-plated backs and from the mudguard stays.

Carpet is fitted on the floor of the driving compartment, and the dash panel and internal panels are lined. The seats and squab could be a little thicker, and sealing between the various body panels would help eliminate the noise of the suspension working. But these are things the enthusiastic owner would probably undertake while assembling his Seven. When finished he would have a motor car which might lack in comfort but which makes up for it in amusement value a thousand times over; and, moreover, it would be a machine with a safety factor far higher than usual. As a means of learning how to handle a fast car, and at the same time appreciating what really goes on when a car is in motion, the Lotus Seven is hard tobeat. Basic cost of the parts, ready for assembly, is £525, and it is possible to complete the assembly in some 75 hours. An assembled Seven costs £690 to which must be added purchase tax of £346 7s. which raises the total to £1,036 7s. ★

STARK BUT ATTRACTIVE: The sleek lines of the Super Seven are shown to good advantage in this photograph. Weather protection is almost non-existent and the occupants are well advised to wear lots of warm clothing!

The Lotus Super Seven

THE fabulous success story of the marque Lotus started with the construction of special chassis frames for amateur car builders. Having achieved a near-monopoly of certain sports-racing classes, and also entered the Formula 2 and Grand Prix ranks, Colin Chapman has returned to his old love, the do-it-yourself or "Meccano-car". (I am sure that the famous firm of toy manufacturers will forgive me for pirating their title for a moment!)

The basic Lotus Seven is a car that is built round the usual multi-tubular frame, but such expensive features as the all-enveloping streamlined body and the de Dion or independent rear end are deleted. In its cheapest form, the machine is Ford-powered, but the subject of this article is the Super Seven, which has a Coventry Climax engine, type F.W.A. Under certain circumstances, when the parts are bought separately and assembled by a genuine amateur, a special concession operates whereby no purchase tax is levied. Details may be obtained from H.M. Customs and Excise or from Lotus Engineering Co., Ltd., but please don't write to me!

Anyway, feeling that to assemble a car from bits might occupy valuable drinking time, I succeeded in borrowing a complete vehicle. This was the little red job with which Graham Hill secured a most praiseworthy first place at Brands Hatch on Boxing Day, so I knew it was nicely run in. It has a Coventry Climax engine with twin S.U. carburetters, but the normal camshaft, giving 40 degrees of overlap is employed. The camshaft more usually fitted for racing, which gives 60 degrees of overlap, is less pleasant for normal road use. This particular car has an M.G. close-ratio gearbox, a delightful and immensely strong component which is a little heavier than the type most frequently mated to the 1,100 c.c. engine.

CLIMAX POWERED: The Coventry-Climax 1,100 c.c. engine develops 75 b.h.p. at 6,250 r.p.m. The normal camshaft with only 40 degrees overlap is employed on this particular power unit.

For the rest, the typical Lotus frame is fitted with a simple, doorless body. The suspension is by telescopic dampers incorporating helical springs, and although a proprietary rear axle has been adopted, it is positively located on twin trailing arms and a Panhard rod. There is some luggage space in the compartment behind the seats, which also encloses the hood when folded, and the petrol filler cap projects through the plywood bottom. In front, there are strip-type mudguards and separate headlamps, though the radiator is enclosed in a streamlined cowl.

A large man in a leather coat may enter the Super Seven without too much difficulty; getting out requires a good deal more effort. With a well-charged battery, the engine starts readily on even the coldest morning, and does not take long to achieve a working temperature. The noise from the exhaust is not excessive, and the smoothness and willingness to rev. of the Coventry Climax power unit are an absolute joy. The gearchange could not be bettered, and if the competition-type clutch seems fierce at first, it certainly grips at once after a snatched change of ratio. Forty, 60, and 80 m.p.h. can be appreciably exceeded on the indirects, which really does give one a gear for every purpose.

When, some time ago, I tested the first Ford-engined Seven, I must own that I was a little disappointed, and damned it with faint praise in my report. I am delighted to be able to say that an immense amount of development work has taken place since that time, and my two main causes of criticism have been removed. Different brakes have overcome the rather dangerous tendency towards front wheel locking that used to be apparent, and suspension changes, plus a new anti-roll bar, have almost eliminated any tendency for the rear wheels to hop on bumpy corners. The cornering power is very high, and the roadholding is excellent, falling only a little short of that of the more elaborate and costly Lotus models. By more normal standards, the roadholding, steering, and controllability must be rated as superlatively good.

As regards the performance, a 75 b.h.p. engine in a car weighing not much over 8 cwt. must result in some exciting acceleration figures, as the graph and data panel show. The maximum speed is limited by the car's unstreamlined form, but this is of little moment for normal road use or club racing on short circuits. Ninety m.p.h. is available on short straights, but although 100 m.p.h. may eventually be exceeded, this can only be done on a really long straight when the conditions are ideal. Of course, the car tested had a Brands Hatch axle ratio, and may have been running out of revs. on top gear. The brakes are now excellent, and entirely adequate to the

★

FRONT SUSPENSION DETAILS: Telescopic dampers, incorporating helical springs, are used. Drum brakes are standard on this model.

★

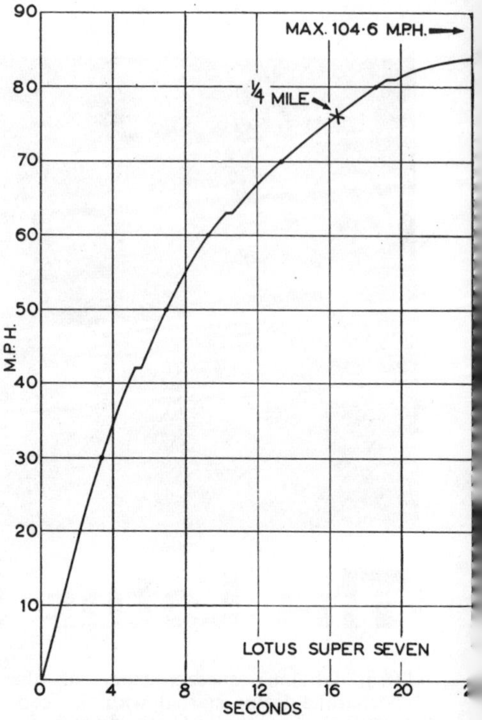

ACCELERATION GRAPH

SPECIFICATION AND PERFORMANCE DATA

Car Tested: Lotus Super Seven sports 2-seater. Price, components £499, power unit £356, bought out £37, total £892, plus extras to choice.

Engine: Four-cylinders 72.4 mm. x 66.6 mm. (1,098 c.c.). Light alloy head and block. Single overhead camshaft driven by straight spur gears and duplex roller chain. Compression ratio 9.8 to 1. 75 b.h.p. at 6,250 r.p.m. Twin SU carburetters. Lucas coil and distributor.

Transmission: Single dry plate clutch. Close-ratio four-speed gearbox with synchromesh on upper three gears and central remote control lever, ratios on test car 4.9, 6.0, 8.2, and 12.2 to 1. Open propeller shaft. Hypoid rear axle.

Chassis: Multi-tubular steel space frame with stressed light alloy shaft tunnel and floor. Independent front suspension by wishbones incorporating torsional anti-roll bar. Rack and pinion steering gear. Live rear axle on twin parallel trailing arms and Panhard rod. Suspension by combined helical springs and telescopic damper units all round. Hydraulic brakes with 8 ins. x 1¼ ins. drums. Knock-on 15 ins. wire wheels fitted 4.50 ins. front and 5.00 ins. rear tyres.

Equipment: 12-volt lighting and starting. Rev. counter, ammeter, water temperature, and oil pressure gauges.

Dimensions: Wheelbase, 7 ft. 4 ins.; track, 3 ft. 11 ins.; overall length, 10 ft. 3 ins.; width, 4 ft. 5 ins. Weight, 8¼ cwt. (approx.).

Performance: Maximum speed 104.6 m.p.h. Speeds in gears: 3rd, 81 m.p.h.; 2nd, 63 m.p.h.; 1st, 42 m.p.h. Standing quarter-mile, 16.4 secs. Acceleration: 0-30 m.p.h., 3.4 secs.; 0-50 m.p.h., 7.0 secs.; 0-60 m.p.h., 9.2 secs.; 0-70 m.p.h., 13.2 secs.; 0-80 m.p.h., 18.4 secs.

Fuel Consumption: 30 m.p.g. (approx.).

speed of the car; the hand-brake is neither particularly convenient nor powerful.

As a road car, the Super Seven is a lot of fun. One sits well down in it, and the protection given by the extra fabric covers over the body cutaways is considerable, avoiding the usual spray of mud up the sleeve. The screen does tend to become dirty when the roads are wet, but more efficient front mudguards are under development. The small headlamps are adequate for reasonable cruising speeds, and may easily be swivelled or dipped for the negotiation of fog. The hood is easy to erect, and is reasonably effective though draughty. In short, the Lotus Super Seven is far from luxurious, but will not by any means be regarded as excessively spartan by the younger sports car enthusiasts. Don't forget that my test took place in the middle of winter!

Even on ordinary workaday journeys, the pleasure of driving a car with a real race-bred engine is very real. Super-tuned versions of mass-produced engines do wonderful work, but may sometimes feel as though they are being hard pressed. The Coventry Climax unit runs up to and past 7,000 r.p.m. with never a murmur of complaint. At cruising speeds, it has a wonderful reserve of power, and the close-ratio gearbox is waiting to be used for sudden bursts of acceleration. Actually, the car is so light that it remains lively if driven largely on top gear. The fuel consumption figure on the data panel is only approximate, and I would expect to average 25 m.p.g. at near-racing speeds and 35 m.p.g. under more reasonable conditions. There was, however, no mileage-recording instrument on the test car, so distances could only be worked out from the map.

As a club racing car, the Super Seven excels. It is fast on short circuits, reliable, and easy to tune and service. It handles so well that it will give every opportunity to the less experienced driver to develop along the right lines. Motor racing can never be a cheap sport, but this car is probably as inexpensive a passport to the game as is at present available. I enjoyed my test very much, even in fog, snow, and ice, but please, Colin, can I have the next open Lotus when the weather is a bit warmer? For further particulars of this car, and of the various items of equipment that are available, please write to the makers at 7 Tottenham Lane, Hornsey, N.8.

Building a Lotus Seven . . .

CONTINUED FROM PAGE 19

sockets is always useful and a power drill makes work easier, along with a good set of files. Any other equipment is sheer luxury, with the possible exception of a torque spanner.

Greatest temptation with all special building is still the same with kit-built cars—that of skimping final detail in order to become mobile. This temptation should be resisted firmly, particularly if any racing is envisaged.

The Lotus kit must be one of the easiest on the market to assemble. I am a valuation surveyor by profession and possess no mechanical genius whatsoever, so I am always surprised when I look at what I have produced.

If intending kit-builders adapt an existing chassis, such as a Ford Anglia or Prefect, to take one of the proprietary shells, more work and much more adaptation will be involved than in producing a Lotus, and certainly a greater total of man-hours.

After completing the car, the next problem is taxing and insuring it. All my own Lotuses have been comprehensively insured for £20 a year, allowing for the no-claims bonus. I have heard stories of some insurance companies asking exorbitant premiums, and frankly this is a case of doing some research until a sensible company is discovered. Some companies will require an engineer's certificate before issuing a cover note, although my own cars have never required one. If the car is well finished, there is nothing to fear.

Having got insurance cover, apply to the local Taxation Office to register the car. They will require all the receipts from the various suppliers to prove that the car is a "one-off" special and not a production machine. This will save the payment of purchase tax.

A man from the Taxation Office will come and look at the car, check the engine and chassis numbers and in due course the registration will arrive, together with receipts suitably stamped by the authority.

This is the story. A considerable sense of achievement, a saving in purchase tax, a 100 per cent knowledge of your own car and the acquisition of a vehicle which is really personal.

JON DERISLEY

HOW TO BUILD A LOTUS SEVEN

By "Sports Car Fan"

ALTHOUGH there is nothing particularly complicated about assembling a Lotus Seven, many people who have built these cars feel that a guide to procedure would be useful. The set of parts is a little bewildering at first sight, and a great deal of work might be done twice over without a plan to follow. With this in mind I have listed the order of assembly together with the components required.

Before starting to put the car together it is best to take stock of the situation. Before delivery the chassis frame and body unit has been fitted with all the brake piping, brake and clutch master cylinders, dash panel and instruments, switches, regulator and fuse box, starter solenoid, stop lamp switch and wiring loom.

Inside the car are fitted the trim panels, while the rear houses the petrol tank and boot floor. The full width glass screen, body badge and rear lamps complete the external fittings.

You will seen then, that the more exacting jobs have already been done. The next step is to divide the components into their respective sections, and this I will do as we cover each stage of construction.

Having set the car at a working height, making sure that the trestles or beer crates are under a frame member and not merely an aluminium panel, remove the bonnet and nose cowling. Unscrew the boot floor and side trims, which are held with self tapping screws, and the tunnel top and body centre section, which are bolted.

Check that the tapped holes in the chassis are clean and then try the correct bolts for it, making sure that you smear graphite grease on them first. Nuts, bolts and washers will be listed after the instructions for the fitting of each component. All threads used are U.N.F. unless otherwise stated.

FRONT SUSPENSION AND STEERING

Components

One pair of wishbones fitted with trunnions and kingposts.
One anti roll bar and mounting blocks.
One pair top arms.
Two suspension units.
Eight bonded rubber half bushes (long).
Two hubs, bearings and caps.
One pair steering arms.
One pair brake assemblies.
Two brake drums.
One rack and pinion and clamps.
Two ball joints.
One steering column and mountings.

1. Assemble each side as a unit, and fit the two-leading-shoe brakes to the kingposts. The bottom bolts screw into the steering arms which are fitted so that the track rod end is on top.

Bolts

Four bolts $\frac{3}{4}$″ x $\frac{5}{16}$″.
Two bolts $1\frac{1}{2}$″ x $\frac{3}{8}$″.
Two bolts $1\frac{1}{4}$″ x $\frac{3}{8}$″.
Two lock tabs.
Four $\frac{5}{16}$″ spring washers.

2. Front hubs; make sure that these are perfectly clean. Pack the inside with grease, of the grade shown on the chassis tag, thumb grease well into the conical inner bearing and place in the hubs.

Tap oil seal retainer into position with the flange to the bearing. Note that the felt seal is squashed between the retainer and kingpost face. Slip hub on to stub pin, push in well greased outer cone bearing, D washer and slotted nuts.

When adjusting the bearings, turn the hub as you tighten the nut. When there is no play, back off the adjustment until the hub is quite free to rotate with the slightest rock. The ideal is .005-.020″ at the wheel rim.

ON NO ACCOUNT LEAVE THE BEARINGS TIGHT.

Split pin the nuts and tap home the grease caps. Fit the suspension units to the wishbones making sure that the tubular spacers are pushed into the rubber eye bushes.

Bolts

Two bolts 2″ x $\frac{1}{2}$″
Two Nyloc nuts.
Four flat washers.

3. Fit the wishbone assemblies using four of the bonded half bushes at the front pick ups.

Bolts

Two bolts 1″ x $\frac{5}{16}$″.
Two spring washers.
Two halfpenny washers.
Two bolts $3\frac{1}{2}$″ x $\frac{1}{2}$″.
Two Nyloc nuts.
Four flat washers.

4. Fit the top arms into the chassis brackets, and the suspension units to the front of the brackets.

Do not forget the tubular spacers in the rubber eye bushes.

Bolts

Two bolts $3\frac{3}{4}$″ x $\frac{1}{2}$″.
Two Nyloc nuts.
Four flat washers.

5. The anti-roll bar ends are cranked down 4 degrees. It is important that the bar is fitted the correct way up, so that the threaded ends are parallel to the ground when the car is at normal ride level.

Use the four remaining bonded half bushes (long) in the top arm eyes.

Bolts

Two Nyloc nuts $\frac{1}{2}$″.
Two flat washers.

Next the split aluminium mounting blocks are bolted to the front of the chassis.

Bolts

Four bolts $1\frac{3}{4}$″ x $\frac{5}{16}$″.
Four spring washers.

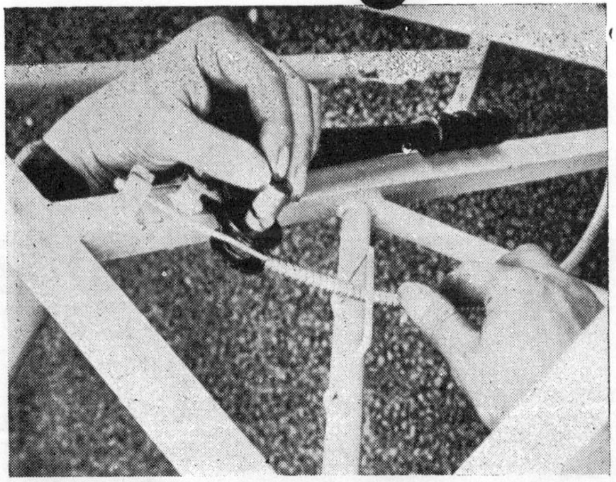

LEFT: Method of Assembly for handbrake lever and cable. BELOW: The rear suspension unit mounting rubbers and caps fitted correctly, i.e., two caps and one rubber below, one cap and one rubber above.

Four flat washers.

Do not finally tighten bolts through rubber bushes until the car is on its wheels and at the correct ride level. This ensures that the bonded bushes are set at their neutral position and are not pre-stressed.

6. Connect brake hoses to bottom wheel cylinders, sealing with copper washers.

7. Fit the rack and pinion loosely with mounting clamps.

Bolts
Four bolts 2¾" x ¼".
Four Nyloc nuts.
Eight flat washers.

Adjust track roughly by eye, making sure that an equal amount of thread is used on both ends.

8. Fit the steering column so that the square bottom bearing is inside the footbox.

Fit the top bearing and, using the bottom bearing as a template, drill the footbox floor.

Fasten with:—
Four bolts ¾" x 3/16".
Five Nyloc nuts.
Ten flat washers.
One bolt 2" x 3/16".

Slip the splined end on to the pinion, noting that the pinch bolt in the universal joint has a particularly long shank.

Turn the rack and pinion up so that the centre universal joint touches the footbox floor; this ensures that the column will not slip off should the pinch bolt come out.

Do not fit the steering wheel until the car is on its wheels and has been tracked. Set the steering in the dead ahead position, check by wheeling the car back and forth, and then fit steering wheel.

This also applies should an alloy steering wheel be fitted, when the aluminium boss must be drilled, using the wheel as a template.
Six countersunk bolts ¾" x 3/16".
Nyloc nuts.
Six flat washers.

REAR SUSPENSION

Components
One rear axle.
One pair top radius arms.
One L.H. bottom radius arm.
One 'A' bracket.
Six bonded rubber half bushes (short).
Two suspension units.

The rear axle must be fitted so that the pinion flange is on the centre line of the tunnel. Adjustment is provided by shim washers between the 'A' bracket and the axle bracket.

The top radius arms curve away from the suspension units and over the axle.

Fit the suspension units with one rubber and two caps below the chassis bracket, and one rubber and one cap above.

Bolts
Two bolts 1" x ½".
Two spring washers.
Two flat washers.

Do not tighten bolts until car is at ride level.

Bolts
Two bolts 2" x ½".
Four bolts 4½" x ½".
Six Nyloc nuts.
Eight flat washers.
Two bolts 1¾" x ⅜".
Two Nyloc nuts.
Four flat washers.
One bolt 1" x 5/16".
One spring washer.
One halfpenny washer.

HANDBRAKE

Components
Handbrake lever.
Handbrake cable.
One barrel.
One Clevis pin.
One split pin.
Bolts
One bolt 2¼" x ¼".
One Nyloc nut.
Two flat washers.

The action is to push the outer cable with the lever.

Run the cable from the axle linkage through the triangular loop in the rear of the tunnel, the centre hole in tunnel gearbox mounting and a slot in the tunnel cover side. Pass the cable through the wire loop by the lever mounting.

With the handbrake lever in position and the slotted barrel placed in the end, run the inner cable through the barrel, which acts as the outer cable stop, and fit the cable and nipple into the square lug on the chassis.

Adjust the brakes by turning the square adjusters on the back plates clockwise until the drum will not turn, and then slacken off until it will revolve freely. Now adjust the handbrake cable.

FUEL LINE

Components
Hose.
Stems and nuts.
'O' clips.

This is run through the gearbox tunnel mounting left hand hole and the triangular loop at the rear. Clip to the undertray at intervals. The 'O' clips are tightened by squeezing each ear with pincers.

PEDALS

Components
One clutch pedal.
One brake pedal.
One throttle pedal.
Two hinges and nuts.

It is necessary to remove the master cylinder mounting bracket to enable the throttle pedal to enter the footbox. The brake and clutch pedals are quite straightforward; use in clevis ends.

Bolts
Two bolts 1" x 5/16".
Two Nyloc nuts.
Four flat washers.

BRAKES

Fit the front drums and wheels. Adjust the front brakes; each shoe has an adjuster which should be turned clockwise until the wheel locks. Slacken off until the wheel spins freely then repeat on the next shoe.

Check that all brake pipe connections are tight.

Bleed the brakes. It may be necessary to do this two or three times, and providing

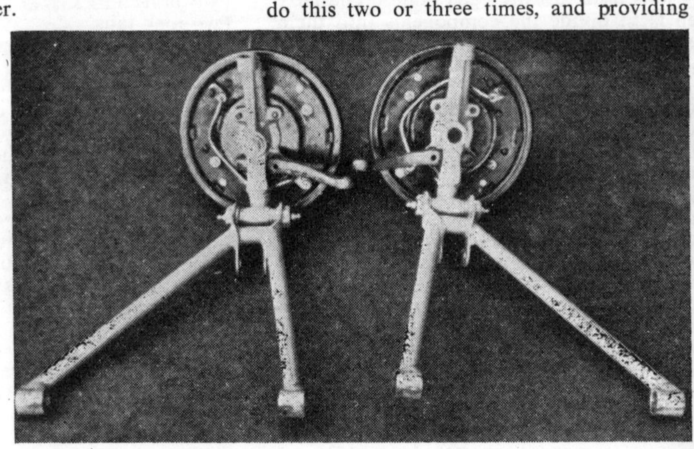

The front wishbones fitted with kingposts and trunnions, steering arms and two-leading-shoe brakes.

the expelled fluid is in a clean container it can be used again after allowing the air bubbles to disperse.

Fit the rear wheels and set the car on the ground.

Check that the suspension is working without fouling by bouncing the car up and down. If all is well the engine can now be fitted.

ENGINE AND GEARBOX

Components

Mounting bar.
Gearbox mounting rubber.
Top water pipe.
Bottom water pipe.
Radiator.
Exhaust pipe.
Silencer.
Propshaft.
SU carburetters and 4 branch manifold if required.

Check that oil filter bolt and all drain plugs are tight.

Remove the fan as this is not necessary.

Replace oil pressure switch with $\frac{1}{8}$" B.S.P. union body, sealing with a fibre washer.

Check that propshaft fits the gearbox tail shaft spline. Lay propshaft inside the tunnel but do not bolt to the pinion flange.

Fit speedo cable to gearbox. Slip rubber grommet on gearbox tailshaft casing with flat to the top. Lubricate the grommet with soft soap.

It is as well to protect the forward engine bay cross tube with a piece of slit rubber hose before fitting the engine.

Have two 2" x $\frac{7}{16}$" bolts ready to slip into the front mountings, and then lift the engine and gearbox into the car.

Fit the tunnel bracket clamp.
Two Nyloc nuts $\frac{5}{16}$".
Two flat washers.

Fit the flexible steel oil pipe to the $\frac{1}{8}$" B.S.P. union and run the pipe back horizontally to the bulkhead. Drill a $\frac{3}{8}$" diameter hole in the bulkhead next to the vertical tunnel tube and fit the pipe, using the thin lock nut. Screw on the conical end of the plastic oil pipe and run up to the oil pressure gauge, where a leather washer is fitted between the flat end of the pipe and the gauge.

Connect speedo cable.

Connect water temperature bulb to cylinder head.

Fit coil.

Bolts

Two bolts 1$\frac{3}{4}$" x $\frac{1}{4}$".
Two Nyloc nuts.
Four flat washers.

Connect leads to starter, dynamo, coil and distributor.

Fit exhaust pipe, using Ford clamp, to manifold.

Fit silencer to exhaust pipe with a Jubilee clip.

Note the 4 degree crank of the anti-roll bar end. Both bars are the correct way up.

Bolts

Two bolts 2" x $\frac{5}{16}$".
Two spring washers.
Two flat washers

Connect hose to clutch slave cylinder and bleed, using brake fluid.

THROTTLE LINKAGE

Components

One cable.
One cable stop.
One clevis clip.
One pin.
One spring.
One clip.
One bolt 1" x $\frac{3}{16}$"
One Nyloc nut.
One flat washer.

Remove the cranked Solex throttle arm and straighten in a vice. Remove the ball from the arm by filing the burred over end. Refit the arm to the carburetter. Fit the return spring clip to the nearest manifold stud. Replace the existing bolt holding the choke cable clamp with the 1" x $\frac{3}{16}$" bolt.

Fit the cable stop bracket on the bolt and fasten with Nyloc nut and flat washer. Fit clevis clip to throttle arm with pin and fit return spring in pin hole and clip. Fit the cable between the cable stop and throttle pedal arm. The inner cable fits in a bracket on the lower frame member below the arm.

A plate is welded on the throttle arm to act as a return stop; this may need filing to position the pedal.

Fit throttle cable and clips.

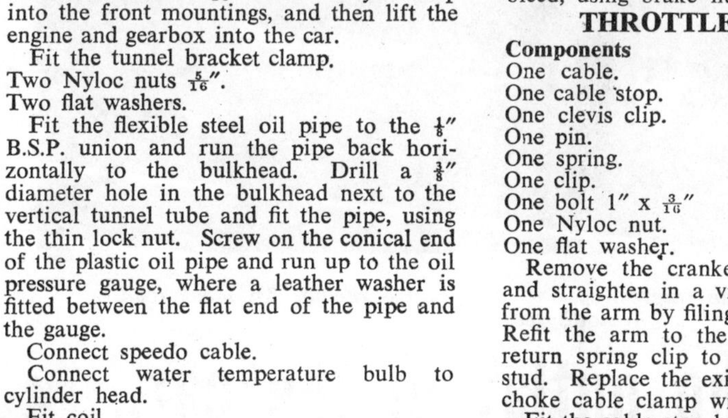

Close - up of the front wishbone assemblies and two - leading - shoe brakes.

TWIN CARBURETTERS

Components

Two SU carburetters H2.
Two stub pipes.
Two gaskets.
Four bolts 1" x $\frac{3}{8}$".
Four Nyloc nuts.
Eight flat washers.
One mounting plate.
Four bolts 1" x $\frac{5}{16}$".
Four Nyloc nuts.
Eight flat washers.
One bonded rubber stud c/w nuts and washers.
One length petrol resisting hose.
Four Jubilee clips.
Two ball joints.
Four $\frac{3}{16}$" plain nuts.
One length $\frac{3}{16}$" studding.
Two spring washers.

Bolt carburetters to mounting plate and line them up with the inlet stubs. Drill a $\frac{1}{4}$" dia hole in line with hole in the chassis bracket.

Temporarily fit the bonded rubber stud, so that the stub pipes and rubber hose can be cut to length. Do not have a greater gap than $\frac{1}{2}$" between the two stub pipe ends.

Fit together with Jubilee clips. Make up throttle link to your liking, using the $\frac{3}{16}$" studding and ball joints.

Cut throttle return spring to size and form end loops. Complete assembly by synchronising both carburetters and fitting the link and spring.

Fit choke cable. Fit side entry distributor cop. Place radiator in position, using the 'top hat' rubber grommets on the mounting pegs. Drill $\frac{1}{4}$" dia hole through the aluminium baffle plate in front of the radiator, using as a guide the lug soldered to the bottom tank.

Bolt together fitting a rubber grommet between the two.

Bolts

One bolt $\frac{3}{4}$" x $\frac{1}{4}$".
One Nyloc nut.
Two flat washers.

The fore and aft position of the radiator is located by the top water pipe.

Bolts

One bolt 2" x $\frac{1}{4}$" UNC.
One bolt $\frac{3}{4}$" x $\frac{1}{4}$" UNC.
Two spring washers.
Two flat washers.

(Continued on page 23)

The Lotus Seven needs little or no modification to provide interesting and competitive racing. An ideal road car, its specialty is Traffic Light GPs, though the girl-friend might not agree.

For little more than the outlay of the car..

YOU CAN RACE A LOTUS SEVEN

...and be competitive

By ROBERT GRANT

HOW many sports cars can one buy for under £1500 and race straight off with a reasonable chance of success? The Lotus Seven is one of the few that fits the bill. This can be modified but that entails further outlay — so let's leave it as it is. The smaller version, costing £1200, of the diminutive Seven is powered by a 997 cc Ford motor and its younger and more powerful brother, the Super Seven, is priced at £1395 with its 1498 cc motor delivering 95 bhp.

There are other vehicles which can be put onto a circuit straight from the showroom. However, the Seven has the edge on them since it is stark, light and built by a firm with vast racing experience. The Sprite at £1059 is easily adapted for racing but not without the aid of a generous amount of roubles.

The Datsun Fairlady has yet to make its racing debut, which speaks for itself. Both the MGB and the Spitfire come under the £1500

Standard LOTUS can win you races!

price range but then there are far quicker cars in the class.

It is obvious that the Lotus Seven is the most promising from road to track and/or both.

The phrase "Motor racing is an expensive business" is a worn one but alas quite true. As each season progresses, so does the expense. Therefore if you want to win motor races you do require a more than average income. The obvious answer to this is to get a sponsor but no one in their right mind will sponsor anyone until they have proof positive of driving ability in the form of race results. It has been said that one's first season's motor racing can be the most expensive. There is a deal of truth in this for, without experience, mistakes come easily both in race technique and race preparation.

You have your Lotus Seven which is either bought ready-built or in kit form. The car should be bought in the latter state not only from the expense angle but if you construct the car yourself the better you'll know it and logically drive it.

To race a Lotus Seven, or any other car, it is essential to prepare two things. First the car and secondly yourself. We will deal with the former to start with.

Remove the present heavy, wind resisting screen and replace it with a small curved perspex racing screen. The bonnet catches on the Seven are not 100 percent reliable and it is upsetting having to pit to secure them. Prevent this by fitting two small leather straps on each side of the bonnet. I don't know how wide the average Australian posterior is but I certainly found that when cornering I would slide from side to side in the seat. The answer to this is to jam a large lump of foam rubber either side of you or, better still, fit a seat from an open-wheeler. A small fire extinguisher should be bolted to the scuttle.

Tyre pressures, carburetion, oil, plug and fuel gradings can be sorted with experience. But listen to other competitors and those who know for hints. The standard brake linings are adequate but keep an eye on them. A complete strip down after every few races is essential if you want your motor to last. Besides you'll want to sell it when you're offered your works drive! Take with your car spare cans of fuel and oil (unless available at the circuit) and a spare set of plugs. A comprehensive tool kit is vital and it deserves to be kept in a concertina type tool box. A good trolley jack is a must.

Next on the agenda is you. You are the human element in the combination. Your attitude is the most important; thoroughness and dedication are the prime needs. The good old boot-on-the-floor hell-for-leather-type doesn't get very far. Before you even buy your own car you can learn simply by spectating and watching other drivers' lines and techniques.

There are several very good books from which one can learn a lot, such as Denis Jenkinson's "The Racing Driver" or Paul Frere's "Competition Driving". You do not need a competition licence to attend a Racing Drivers' School. If you do and scare yourself stupid, then think again.

First step on to the track proper is to join a club, the best example in NSW being the AARC, or the club in your area. Then, provided your driving licence is in order, you apply to CAMS for your provisional racing licence accompanying this with the correct medical certificate.

CONTINUED ON PAGE 23

To become competitive the Sprite, though cheap, demands considerable outlay on tuning work and suspension modification.

Frank Matich scored many successes in the Elfin Clubman. Similar to the Seven in looks and characteristics the Elfin avoids import tax the Lotus suffers.

Both the Seven and the Super Seven can be bought in kit form. The former's Ford power unit produces 45 bhp and the latter's 95 bhp.

DO-IT-

Everything that is needed to go motoring. Complete kit for a Lotus Seven

A REVIEW OF CAR KITS AND BODIES FOR AMATEUR CONSTRUCTION

WHILE a number of years ago "special building" was very much in the hands of knowledgeable enthusiasts, and two amateur constructions rarely looked the same, the situation in the last two years has altered radically. It was not unnatural that, with a "do-it-yourself craze" pervading most everyday tasks, it should catch on with special building.

There are obvious and sound reasons for this. First a remarkably high percentage of people are interested in mechanical contrivances, and most car kits fulfil adequately any yearnings to play with Meccano outfits (but do not call for the skill required in building from scratch). Secondly, and more importantly, the anomalies of the British tax system offer the amateur car builder a considerable saving in purchase tax. There are now in the United Kingdom about 40 different firms offering build-it-yourself car kits. This range is very complete and covers almost all tastes, depth of pocket, mechanical skill and time available. Developments of plastic-reinforced glass fibre have given a great fillip to the industry.

Simplest unit is that sold by Auto Bodies; they claim that the only modification required to a Ford Popular chassis before fitting their body is a slight lowering of the radiator. In most cases, manufacturers recommend the boxing in of the chassis members in order to make the frame more rigid. However, it would appear that the day of the Ford Popular and Austin Seven chassis, which have proved so popular with the special builders—partly no doubt because of their cheapness and availability—is possibly on the wane. Many kit manufacturers are now offering at least a simple space frame or tubular ladder type chassis. Even so, the Ford chassis has left its mark, and most bodies are designed for 7ft 6in. wheelbases.

In the more complicated chassis class is the L.M.B.; for a number of years Leslie Ballamy has been applying his theories on suspension to Ford Populars, and achieving remarkable results. He has now developed a lightweight chassis using his system. An agreement has been reached between L.M.B. Components, and E.B. (Staffs) Ltd., who manufacture the Debonair body, to combine their products.

There is a wide choice in the field of complete cars, and a prospective customer probably will be able to fill his particular needs. In the open car range there are Turner, Fairthorpe, Lotus and Yimkin, all excellent buys for the man who wishes to go club racing. Tornado cars did well last year, winning the six-hour relay race at Silverstone, Falcon have introduced an open competition model, and a promising showing was made in races last season by the G.S.M. Delta. Ashley, Falcon, Gilbern and G.3 Ginetta are the answer for those who prefer a little more comfort and a roof over their heads. Both Tornado and Conversion Car Bodies offer estate car type bodies.

Choice of engines is restricted mainly to Ford 100E and 105E, B.M.C. A-type, and Standard 10. Coventry Climax FWE and FWA, MGA, Triumph TR3 and larger Ford engines also appear in the lists. Most firms offer improved performance engines. Naturally, the better the workshop facilities at the disposal of the constructor, the easier will be his task. On the other hand, as one of the authors of two articles in this issue says, a bare minimum is all that is

YOURSELF CARS

absolutely necessary. For the construction of the Gilbern, the manufacturers list the following tools as essential; set of spanners, screwdriver (including one Phillips type), a good car-lifting jack, some large wooden blocks or strong boxes, a roll of masking tape, and a ¼in. electric drill (a hand drill will do as no metal parts need boring). All firms supply instruction books on how to assemble their car; particularly comprehensive ones are published by Tornado and Gilbern, and Super Accessories sell booklets on Ford and Austin special building, which provide all the information on the subject that the tyro might need.

The length of time it takes to build any particular kit rests entirely with the builder, his speed of working and the care he takes. Lotus claim that their Seven can be constructed in 12 hours. Final results naturally will depend on the ability of the constructor, and the patience he is willing to exercise. Of course, certain manufacturers offer better basic material than others, and in this particular field price is no criterion by which to judge. It has been noticed that not even the producers of some kits have always managed to build a well-finished final product themselves. On the other hand, manufacturers say that most complaints received are from people who fail to follow assembly instructions correctly.

Building a Lotus Seven

Too much thought about the amount of equipment and knowledge needed to build one's own car from a kit of parts might well deter some people, but while both these would make the job easier they are not necessary.

I have been concerned with the construction of seven Lotuses of various types, three of which have been my own. Each of the trio ras been raced, and the first pair had to do duty as shopping cars and general hacks when not being raced.

Above: Jon Derisley's Lotus leads a more streamlined model through a bend at Brand's Hatch. Right: Twin Weber carburettors are used on the Ford 105E fitted in this Lotus VII

First thing to decide is for what purpose the car is going to be used; as a road car pure and simple, a sports-racing car or an out-and-out racer. Having decided this point, it is necessary to do some very careful costing, with the aid of various manufacturers' price lists, to find out if the project will be acceptable to your bank manager.

Once you (or he) have (has) decided that you can afford to build the car, the next problem is "Can I do it?" In the early days, some kits on the market were sketchy indeed and quite a large amount of home fabrication was needed. Now, however, the whole process has been tidied up. The latest Lotus VII, which I built just before Christmas, was collected from the works on a Friday afternoon. That evening the chassis was in place on two trestles and the suspension arms, springs and shock absorber units laid out on the floor. All other parts were laid out on shelves ready for assembly.

Work started on Saturday morning, and with the help of a friend, the car was standing on its own wheels that evening. On Sunday afternoon the car was ready to receive the engine. On Monday evening, two more friends helped with the installation of the engine, and the next four evenings were spent in adding the carburettors, exhaust system, transmission and plumbing for the cooling system. By Friday evening the wiring had been fitted and the next morning the car was started and driven round the block.

Assembly could have been carried out even more quickly, but I am a great believer in making haste slowly. My own feeling is that the Lotus comes with far too much done by the works before the customer takes over. The chassis-body unit has the brake lines and wiring loom already installed. Boxes contain all the bits and pieces for the home constructor, which all seem very puzzling at first but soon become obvious as work progresses. All necessary nuts, bolts and washers are supplied.

The first Lotus I built was finished in the open with a screwdriver, pliers and an adjustable spanner, as well as two files. Basically, all that is needed is a good bench and vice, sets of open-ended and ring spanners and other small tools. A set of

CONTINUED ON PAGE 12

Meet a car that's easy to drive and can be assembled in your backyard.

LOTUS WITH

LOTUS people are probably the most individualistic car manufacturers in the world. Guided by a near-genius with the energy of a reactor and the directiveness of a guided missile, they put out an astonishing range of sporting and racing machinery. Colin Chapman is as sage a businessman as he is an engineer. He aims his bread and butter machinery at the mass market, using proprietory parts (where available), to keep the cost down to reasonable levels. But he buys his publicity with remarkably ingenious racing cars, built at considerable expense.

In the case of the Lotus Seven, the car is available either off the assembly lines or in kit form, to be built at home. According to the factory, it takes between 80 and 100 man hours to assemble a kit, using nothing more elaborate than a power drill and a set of car tools. As a promotion stunt, a team of Lotus men managed to bolt a Seven together in a few hours in the New York Motor Show, but the average owner can expect to put in two or three week ends on the job.

In many ways Colin Chapman can be compared to Ettore Bugatti. His original approach to designing, his refusal to take anything for granted and his ability to enthuse owners with a respect amounting to fervor, are all reminiscent of the maestro. So, too, is the fact that Chapman always sacrifices comfort for lightness.

Small though it is, another similarity is that in common with Bugatti, Chapman does not keep his Type numbers in strict chronological order. The Lotus Seven, for example was produced some time after the Eight, which was the first of the aerodynamic Lotus models.

Why then does he continue to market what to some people is an old fashioned body design, when a more effective envelope body could be produced at a comparable cost?

The answer lies in the fact that the Lotus Seven is a dual purpose vehicle. It is a sports racing car in the true sense of the word. It does not pretend to compete with other British two-seaters, which are designed more as touring roadsters than strict sports cars. It is intended to form the basis of an effective racing car without a great deal more expense.

With fuel and spare wheel aboard, the Seven weighs only 8 cwt. It is available with a choice of three engines — BMC, Ford or Coventry Climax. All three units can be modified, if required, to turn the Seven into a true competition car. For example, in its standard form the BMC "A" series motor develops 37 bhp, but one Australian enthusiast has already boosted this power to a genuine 82 bhp, using almost every trick in the book.

Sixty bhp is by no means an over-ambitious target for this 945 cc motor and it goes without saying that an engine of this power in a two-seater weighing only 8 cwt will produce a quite exceptional sports-racing car at a modest cost.

Although the Lotus Seven stands knee high to almost anything you

The BMC A series motor in the du Cros Lotus.

By PEDR DAVIS

SPLIT PERSONALITY

care to name, it is by no means difficult to get into. This much we learned during a recent visit to Beacon Hill near Sydney where we drove the first Lotus Seven to come to NSW.

It is owned by Mrs Wendy Du Cros and was imported in kit form. Her husband, Edward, aided by Keith Watts assembled the kit and the trio has now formed a racing stable, intending to enter the Seven in circuit and hill climb events. The other cars in the group include a Borgward and a very swift Peugeot.

The kit cost £1245 (in Sydney) including tax, which is at a lower rate than for a fully assembled motor vehicle. Thus, in price, the Lotus falls conveniently between the Sprite and an MG.

It is not a suitable vehicle for the man who merely wants fast transport because it is lacking in many of the home comforts found with most factory produced sports cars. The all-weather equipment keeps out the rain, but not the wind; the seats are comfortable but non-adjustable; the headlights

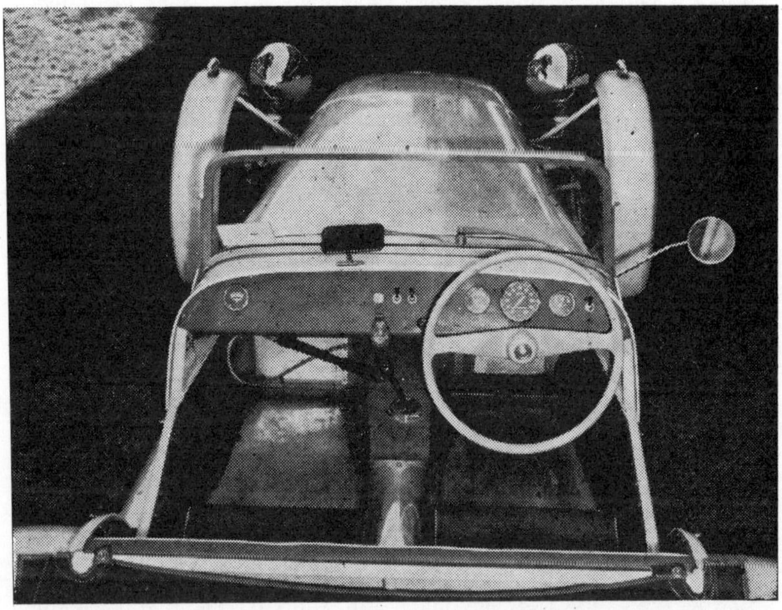

The cockpit, with handbrake resting against the passenger's knee.

The Seven equipped for the weather with Australian-designed side screens, like the Goggo Dart. But entry and exit is a real problem.

LOTUS WITH SPLIT PERSONALITY Cont.

are adequate rather than impressive, and the exhaust has a fruity tone which could be heard by a policeman standing two blocks away.

But for the man who enjoys his motoring, who likes to live with his machine and who demands a high standard of safety with zestful performance, the Seven stands out way ahead of the field.

There is nothing complicated or exotic about the design. The multiple space frame is clad in a stressed aluminium body with a fibreglass nose cone and separate fibreglass mudguards. The engine is mounted at the front and drives a proprietory rear axle through a conventional transmission system. All four wheels are sprung on combined coil and damper units and rely on normal 8 in hydraulic brake drums, unless discs are specified as optional extras.

The current choice of engine lies between the A series BMC unit, a Ford Anglia (ohv), a Ford Ten (side valve) and the 1100 cc Coventry Climax unit. The latter is by no means easy to get because of production limitations and it is not likely that many will be seen here.

The Du Cros car is fitted with the BMC engine. It had only been assembled a few days before we drove it, consequently a full road test was out of the question. (We hope later to have this opportunity when the engine has been suitably modified). However, the Seven is not expected to give a startling performance in stock form.

Acceleration for the stock Ford version is quite creditable, with a standard quarter in 21.2 sec and 0-60 mph in 16.2 sec. Fuel consumption, once again influenced by the lack of streamlining, is not exciting for an 8 cwt car, working out at 38 mpg at a constant 40 mph.

This, of course, is an answer to anyone who argues that aerodynamics are over-rated. Lotus have built cars capable of 61 mpg at a constant 40 mph. The 1100 cc Mk IX is an example. Even at a constant 60 mph, its mileage worked out at 49.0 mpg. Maximum speed was 113 mph, from a 72 bhp Coventry Climax unit.

The compact dimensions of the Seven make it particularly useful in traffic. Overall length is a mere 11 ft, width 4 ft 5 in and wheelbase 7 ft 4 in. Although the height to the top of the scuttle is only 27½ in, the minimum ground clearance is 5 in. The turning circle is a fantastic 24 feet to the left and 30 feet to the right.

When assembled from the kit, the body is a dashing mixture of gleaming aluminium and red impregnated fibreglass. Like many owners, the Du Cros sprayed theirs a more suitable color for road use.

Two features of the car are disappointing. One is the all-weather equipment. In standard form, it consists of a pair of hoops with a plastic top that normally sits behind the front seats. This top fastens into place with quick action studs. No side screens are provided, so Edward Du Cros had a pair specially made up, based on Bill Buckle's Goggo screens. They were very necessary, too, because the Lotus front wheels throw up rain water with gay abandon.

The second disappointment concerns the headlights. In standard form, the Lotus is built to comply with safety regulations by fitting a permanently deflected Lucas fog lamp on the left and a Lucas long-range driving lamp on the right. In Britain this is legal provided the right-hand lamp is switched off when traffic approaches and the wing mounted parking lamp remains aglow.

But even if the arrangement would pass Australian traffic authorities, it has little to commend it. Therefore Edward Du Cros fitted a pair of dipping head lamps from an MG TC.

The instrument panel is neat and effective. An excellent view of the dials can be seen through the two spoked steering wheel. The speedometer is calibrated to 100 mph (?) and the three other dials are for the ammeter oil pressure gauge and water temperature gauge. Actually the Seven engine appears to run unnecessarily cool, despite the limited radiator opening. For this reason, Edward Du Cros fitted the number plate across the grille but even this did not bring the temperature up to normal working levels.

Of course after the engine has been suitably modified, it is likely that the cooling system will require no changes to cope with the extra heat.

The suspension system is a classic of simplicity.

CONTINUED ON PAGE 23

Owner Mrs Wendy du Cros in the Lotus, with its stablemate Borgward in the background.

LOTUS WITH A SPLIT PERSONALITY

CONTINUED FROM PAGE 22

The IFS uses transverse wishbones with an anti-sway bar and a pair of combined coil springs and telescopic dampers. The rear suspension has a BMC "A" series axle, located by twin parallel trailing arms and a diagonal member to provide lateral location. Coil springs with in-built dampers are also used.

Nine inch brake drums provide very powerful stopping, because of the low all-up weight. Disc brakes are available as optional extras, so are wire wheels.

In the first series Lotus Sevens, the battery was located at the back for weight distribution reasons. Now a lightweight battery (24 lbs) is placed behind the engine. The fuel tank has also been reduced in size to five gallons, so as to augment the luggage space.

Roadholding gives extraordinarily good cornering power and though the springing is understandably firm, the ride is not uncomfortable. Body roll just does not exist and the car handles with the sureness and confidence of a thoroughbred. It is eminently safe, and provides remarkably enjoyable motoring.

The Lotus Seven is classed as a production sports car and can enter races in this category. But because of its lack of streamlining, it is obviously best suited to short circuits and hill climbs. In Britain, it is a most popular car for mud trials, known as scrambles, where a unique type of motoring has been brought to a thrilling perfection.

For those owners who wish to convert the Seven into competition trim, Lotus market a wide range of optional extras, including a banana exhaust system, close ratio gearbox and non-standard rear axle ratios.

Australian enthusiasts will have noted that their £1245 buys basic sports car specifications. But actually, it buys more. The Seven is a dual purpose vehicle. Apart from its sporting nature, it is a genuine racing car, particularly suitable for the novice and then equally suited (with a much modified engine) for the experienced man. It can be driven to and from a race track without using a trailer and offers alternative transport for weekend or even for day-to-day motoring.

You have only to sit in the cockpit to realise that it is a true sports car, with no concessions to comfort. The driving controls are placed for rapid action, apart from the handbrake. This is located above the passenger's knee, a starting point for many conversations without doubt. Because of the high power to weight ratio, top gear is most flexible and it is only necessary to use the gearbox if a really brisk performance or maximum cornering power is needed.

SUMMING UP:. The lotus Mk Seven is a quite delightful unusual type of sports car, appealing to the section of the market that demands a traditional sports car with the temperament of a true racer. #

CONTINUED FROM PAGE 17

Without the last two items, plus a crash hat, you will not get farther than the scrutineers. Personal equipment should include a good pair of goggles or visor and shoes which don't have edges that catch on the pedals or rubber soles that slip on oil, plus an approved crash helmet. Smart fire-proof overalls don't make you go faster but do protect you.

Right, now you are all prepared and at the circuit. Walk round the track first and note lines and markers for braking and exit points bearing in mind that if it happens to rain, these will be radically different. The AARC provides practice days which are most useful for this purpose and for also getting the feel of the event proper. Take with you a reliable friend who won't spend the time gazing at the women and who can be counted on to note all your lap times. Keep the times in a book, together with the conditions under which they were made and the tyre pressures, spring rates and plug types. This is both a good reference and guide to improvements on your times.

Your first race meeting arrives. Get to all the various sessions early, i.e. scrutineering, practice and the race itself. Get stick-on numbers — they are cheaper — but take them OFF before you leave. During practice remember the points you chose and above that you're a learner, so follow someone else who knows better.

You've completed all practice and preparation. Don't worry about roll bar thicknesses and camber angles just yet. The Lotus Seven is the ideal car to start on so keep it on the island and you'll be OK.

You're on the grid now so it's up to you — and don't take too much notice of the chap who advises you to take such-and-such a corner flat out in top. #

How to Build a Lotus Seven

CONTINUED FROM PAGE 15

Fit bottom water pipe with angle hose to radiator.

Fit the propshaft.

Bolts

Four bolts 1" x 5/16"
Four Nyloc nuts.

The remote gear control can then be fitted into the tunnel and fastened with
Six bolts 1/2" x 3/16".
Six Nyloc nuts.
Six flat washers.
for which you must drill 3/16" holes in the tunnel sides.

Cut a hole in the tunnel cover for the gear lever. Cut a 3" dia hole in the centre section with a slit to the edge and fit the rubber boot to control rod.

Fit horn.

Bolts

Two bolts 3/4" x 3/16".
Two Nyloc nuts.
Four flat washers.

Fit battery.

The suspension bolts can now be tightened.

Set front wheel track to 1/8" toe in at hub height.

Fit steering wheel.

Fit the front wings and stays with the headlamp mountings to the rear, allowing for full bump clearance inside the wings.

Bolts

Eight bolts 1 1/4" x 3/16".
Eight Nyloc nuts.
Sixteen flat washers.
Eight bolts, special coach.
Eight plain nuts.
Eight flat washers.

Drill wings for side lamps.

Run wires through wing stays and connect to side lamps.

Fit headlamps, noting that in the dipped position the offside lamp is switched off.

The number plate lamp is mounted on the "D" shaped plate which is in turn bolted to the rear number plate.

Bolts

Two bolts 1" x 3/16".
Two 3/16" Nyloc nuts.
Four 3/16" flat washers.
Two bolts 1/2" x 5/32"
Two plain nuts.
Two spring washers.

READY FOR THE ROAD

Lubricate all grease nipple points.

Fill engine, gearbox and rear axle with their respective oils.

Fill water system.

Set the tyre pressures to 20 lb sq in front and rear.

On starting the engine check that there is oil pressure, that the dynamo is charging and look for oil and water leaks.

Adjust the carburetter. If you have 2 SUs requiring synchronisation, the Lotus Works will be pleased to provide tuning instructions.

After a short road test check again for leaks.

The running-in speed can be as high as 45 mph in top gear.

When you have completed 500 miles replace all oils and check over nuts and bolts.

The weather proofing can be improved by filling all pop rivets and joints which are subject to wetness with Sealastic or a similar preparation. Obviously it is preferable to do this before assembling the car.

If you plan to paint the car yourself, it is as well to remember to use an etching primer before filler coats and colour.

The Autocar road tests

A pleasing mixture of the modern and the traditional, the Super Seven sports racing model is, above all, light and simple

LOTUS SUPER SEVEN

No. 1853

FEW cars more functional than the Lotus Super Seven have come our way for test, and few have proved as exhilarating to drive. Priorities were clearly established for its design—performance, simplicity, low price—and they have been observed; acceleration and speed are outstanding by any standards, and the handling is provided to match them. Only the bare essentials of a roadable car are provided and the price in component form for final assembly by the owner is £599.

In fairness to both the Super Seven in one sense, and to other sports cars in another, it is right to think in terms of a racing car made usable on the ordinary roads. There is just the minimum of equipment, trim and passenger comforts, the suspension is hard and the exhaust note somewhat shattering at the middle and higher r.p.m. range. Only the young and lithe can slide into the driving seat with ease and decorum. Despite these qualifications, the Super Seven cannot fail to please the enthusiast.

The complete car weighs just a few pounds over $8\frac{1}{2}$ cwt. A multi-tubular space frame supports simple aluminium panels; glass fibre is the material of the nose and wings; there are no doors, and the engine cover lifts clear off four catches. A plywood shelf over the fuel tank gives a shallow, rectangular compartment in which to carry light luggage, tools, hood and covers. The spare wheel is strapped almost vertically on the back. Lamps are provided, of course, but not bumpers, and the horn is scarcely audible. The flat screen and the other road equipment are bolted on and can be removed easily for competition driving. This is a car to drive to a club race meeting, race and drive home again.

A proprietary live rear axle with 4 to 1 final drive ratio is employed; at the front are transverse wishbones and an anti-roll bar. Combined coil-spring and damper units are fitted all round.

Space is adequate in the cockpit but obviously there is no surplus. With two large people in the seats, elbow room is limited; for a driver alone, the position is comfortable with a good stretch of the legs to the pedals—themselves rather close together—and the steering wheel is well set for angle and reach. The gear lever is splendid; some 6in. long, it permits gears to be changed with no more than a wrist movement, the driver's forearm resting on the top of the high transmission tunnel. Gear changes are exceptionally quick, precise and easy to make, but a little care may be needed to avoid snicking reverse when shifting quickly from first to second.

Owners of kit cars of this nature make adjustments to seating and minor controls and instruments to suit themselves. Simple padded vynyl-covered seats are provided, which rest on the floor and wedge between the tunnel and the car sides. An extra seat cushion in the form of 1in. thick foam rubber was found to add to the comfort over rough roads without raising the passengers too high. Like the seats themselves, the occupants are firmly located at the hips. Some form of rest for the clutch foot would be appreciated.

In front of the driver is mounted the r.p.m. indicator, flanked by the oil pressure and water temperature dials. The speedometer is away to the left and the switches, including one for the electric cooling fan, in the middle. Obviously these could all be rearranged to suit individual taste. A parking brake lever is mounted horizontally over the passenger's knees. The small rear-view mirror is a feeble thing—poorly placed and given to vibration blur, so we removed it and fitted a Barnacle near the top centre of the screen.

Since all control movements are short and the steering is high geared ($2\frac{3}{4}$ turns from lock to lock), a driver unfamiliar with such a car may at first handle it jerkily and overcontrol. With a little practice, handling can become unusually smooth and precise. The steering lock of only 29ft average is very good.

Response to throttle movement by the Cosworth converted 1,340 c.c. Ford 109E engine is instantaneous and eager, twin

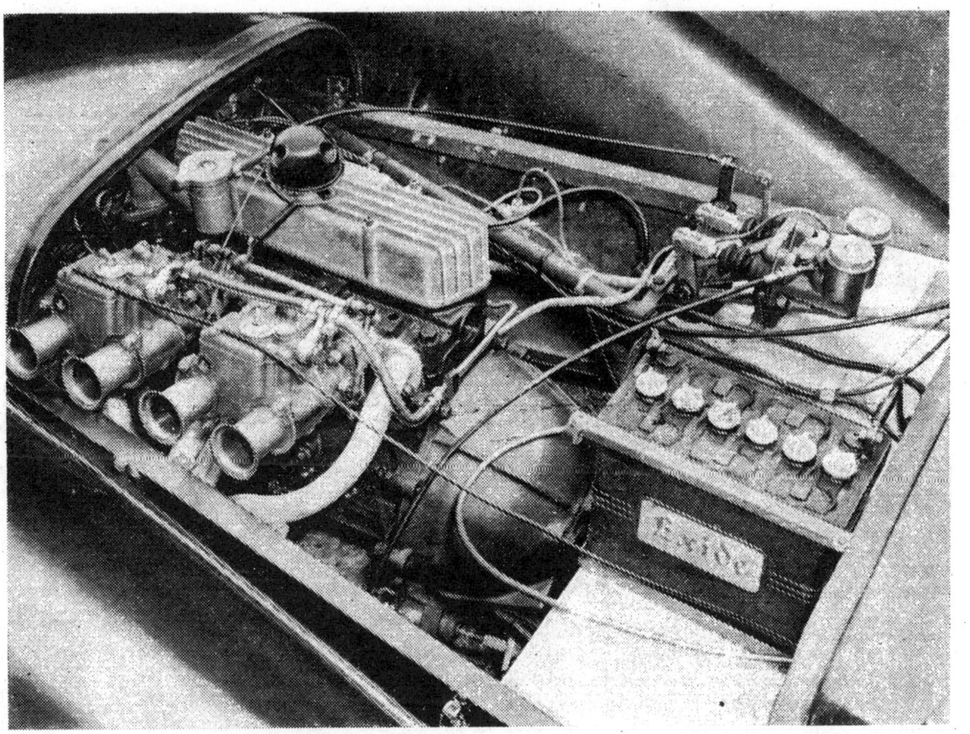

Basically a 1,340 c.c. Ford Classic engine, this unit is much modified by Cosworth. Note the twin Weber carburettors and the special exhaust pipes. There is no radiator header tank, only an extended filler pipe

Weber carburettors being fitted to the test car. Cold starting is easy and requires the use of choke only for a few seconds. Starting troubles early in our test were traced to plug faults and flooding of a carburettor. The car moves away smoothly and easily in bottom gear without abnormal employment of clutch or r.p.m. If maximum get-away is wanted, 3,000-4,000 r.p.m. can be used without the clutch appearing to suffer. So light is the car that wheel spin is very easily provoked on moist or wet roads, in all the intermediate ratios; in the dry, however, there is scarcely any spin and no axle hop.

The Super Seven reaches normal peak revs of 6,500 very fast indeed, the speeds in the intermediate gears of the close-ratio box being 40, 62 and 84 m.p.h. The changes are a delight, since lever movement is so short, engagement is clean however fast the change is made, and no more than a slight momentary depression of the clutch pedal is needed. The standing quarter-mile figure of 15·8 is one of the best we have recorded and compares with 14·7sec for a good E-type Jaguar and 16·1 for the 300 SL Mercedes tested in 1955.

Despite the degree of tune, this 109E engine remains quite flexible and there is no need for high revs, clutch slipping or continuous gear changing in heavy traffic. The exhaust noise heard from the side-outlet pipe and silencer is no more than sporting up to about 3,000 r.p.m. but it then rises to a clear "blue" note in a way to delight a young enthusiast and horrify the staid and elderly. We drove the car frequently in town, without giving offence—it is a matter for driver restraint.

Although wheelspin greatly reduces acceleration in the wet, the Lotus handles well and safely when it is raining. The adhesion with standard Firestone tyres is good and the quick, light steering permits corrections to be made almost instantaneously. Some friction in the steering column support bush, accompanied by the occasional groan, could no doubt be removed.

Cornering is an experience; the Lotus Seven can be held in control under power to a degree unknown to and unimagined by drivers of ordinary cars. Normally, at recommended tyre pressures, the steering characteristics are neutral. Plenty of power is available to induce oversteer

There is plenty of length to the cockpit and the occupants are firmly located by the transmission tunnel and the body sides

The full all-weather equipment is quite effective, the interior being made reasonably snug and watertight

LOTUS SUPER SEVEN . . .

characteristics (to "hang the tail out" in fact); full power can also be used very early when leaving a corner, without loss of adhesion.

As would be expected, the Lotus makes a ready restart on a one-in-three test gradient and will accelerate rapidly with spinning wheels. The handbrake will also hold the car firmly on the same one-in-three gradient. As a matter of interest, the tractive effort in second gear is among the highest recorded, giving a reading beyond the normal scale of the Tapley meter.

Cruising speed, according to circumstances, is more or less what the driver wants to make it, up to a maximum of about 95 m.p.h. The engine does not seem to be disturbed by continuous operation at high r.p.m., but oil consumption becomes heavy.

For occasional bursts, the makers do not think that over-the-limit r.p.m. will damage the engine; this car was tested to 7,000 r.p.m. without ill effects, though for measuring the performance figures 6,500 was taken as the limit. The all-out maximum speed, screen and hood up, with two passengers and towing a fifth wheel for the independent electric test speedometer, was measured at 103·6 m.p.h. The car was timed over several laps of the banked circuit at the Motor Industry Research Association at a mean speed of 102·7 m.p.h. With racing screen and tonneau cover, and carrying only the driver, we would expect this car to get near to the 110 m.p.h.

Outstanding Acceleration

It will be seen from the tabulated performance figures that the car maintains its very high rate of acceleration up to 90 m.p.h., but thereafter the performance tails off very quickly. This is due in part to engine characteristics but also to drag arising from the simple, chunky shape of the car.

A combination of fantastic acceleration—30 to 60 m.p.h. in 5sec—well-chosen, close gear ratios, and a small agile car, result in journeys being covered very quickly indeed. The driver willingly gives his full concentration to the job, overtaking is quick and safe and good use can be made of the open stretches of road. For long journeys, the fuel tank, which will hold 5½ gallons, is too small, giving a safe range of only about 110 miles, since the last half gallon does not feed. There is neither fuel gauge nor reserve. The engine usually required a pint of oil for each refill of the fuel tank.

It is human to want to "have a go" with a new sporting toy, and *The Autocar* team of drivers are not exceptional in this desire. As a result, the overall fuel consumption recorded is probably on the heavy side. With the twin Webers, a minimum journey figure would be 24 m.p.g. and a best of about 28 m.p.g. should be achieved. The optimum economical cruising speed for motorways is between 50 and 60 m.p.h., when up to 35 m.p.g. should be recorded.

Despite the low weight and hard suspension, the car is not greatly tossed about on indifferent road surfaces and on the straight it holds a steady course without frequent correction. The chassis feels rigid despite its lightness, and suspension movement is confined to short vertical bouncing without any roll or pitch. For touring, it would be reasonable to reduce the tyre pressures by several pounds below the 22 p.s.i. front, 24 rear advised for normal fast driving; this softens the ride without bringing any noticeable unwelcome effects.

Some readers may wonder why drum brakes are fitted (although front discs can be). The answer is that good, cheap proprietary drums, matching the axles, are available and they amply meet the requirements of so light a car, even though designed in the first place for heavier and slower vehicles. The front drums are in the air stream and keep cool.

Pedal movement for the brakes is very short and, like that for the clutch, the operating load is rather high—though not by racing standards. Maximum retardation of 0·85g was obtained at 135lb pedal load; after this, the right front wheel locked. There was some slight residual moisture on the road surface at the time of the test, so a small improvement in this figure may be possible. For fast test driving on road and track, the brakes gave confidence, particularly when applied hard, and no fade was noticed. For ordinary road use, they are perhaps a little insensitive.

For drivers particularly concerned with ordinary motoring comfort and all-weather protection in sports cars, the Lotus Super Seven need not be dismissed from mind. Individual owners could do much to improve the waterproofing and make more lavish the seats, trim and carpeting. A re-circulatory heater is offered and some heat comes back from the engine along the tunnel.

With the hood up, it is very difficult for the driver to insert his legs under the steering wheel, but there is reasonable headroom. The hood frame members do not lie just over the driver's cranium, as in too many sports cars. There is surprisingly little draught round the edges of the flat screen and rain is largely kept out by canvas side covers which fill the cutaway portion of the body sides. Full side screens can also be specified. The main hazard is spray from other vehicles. When one's head is little more than 3ft high—the flat of one's hand can be placed on the road when sitting normally in the car—puddles are close and

The petrol filler cap is not very conveniently positioned in the luggage shelf. The hood cover detaches and the frame folds flat

lorry wheels may tower above. Hood, rear and tonneau covers are attached by studs; many of these worked loose on the test car, owing to vibration and the enlarging of the holes in the aluminium panels.

Headlamps are another fitting which owners would probably alter according to their needs. The car is supplied with the legal complement of lamps, the two heads being, in fact, auxiliaries or spots for other cars. A tumbler switch extinguishes the outside one to "dip." Since they can be twisted or angled on their mountings, they are very good in fog, but there is insufficient spread or range for fast driving at night, particularly if there is even a suggestion of mist or haze.

It will be gathered that the Lotus Super Seven two-seater, when doing the job for which it was designed, is outstandingly good. Obviously there have to be compromises to achieve its remarkable handling and performance, and these are to the detriment of comfort in saloon car terms. The fact that we have felt able to consider it as a roadable sports car is to its credit, and indicates that it is quite able to fill this role. As a vehicle in which to learn to race, it is well mannered, safe and fast, yet the special Ford engine is tractable and should prove reliable, economical and long-lived by competition standards.

Obviously there is a considerable saving for home users who can purchase a construction kit free of purchase tax, but as with all kit-built cars, it would be advisable, after a few hundred miles, to take the finished cars for checking by the manufacturers, since small inaccuracies in steering and suspension geometry have serious effects on handling.

LOTUS SUPER SEVEN

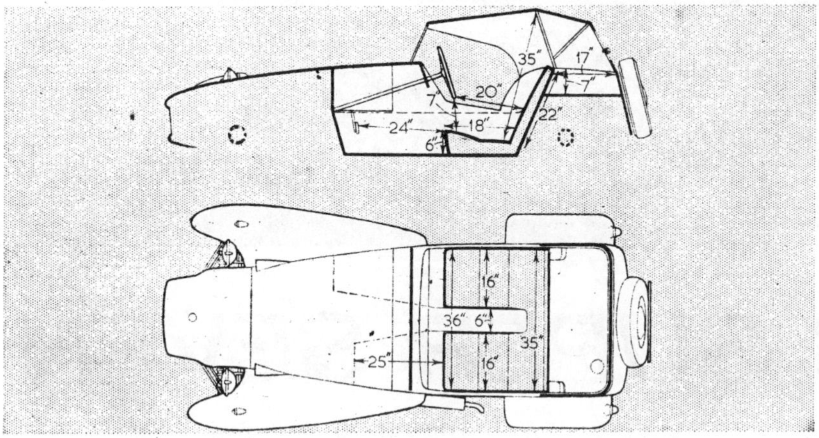

Scale ¼in. to 1ft. Driving seat in central position. Cushions uncompressed.

PERFORMANCE

ACCELERATION TIMES (mean):
Speed range, Gear Ratios and Time in Sec.

m.p.h.	4·11 to 1	5·26 to 1	6·97 to 1	11·99 to 1
10—30 ..	—	5·8	4·2	2·2
20—40 ..	7·9	5·1	3·4	2·4
30—50 ..	6·7	4·4	3·5	—
40—60 ..	6·3	4·3	3·6	—
50—70 ..	8·0	5·0	—	—
60—80 ..	7·6	6·0	—	—
70—90 ..	10·8	—	—	—

From rest through gears to:

30 m.p.h. ..	**2·6 sec**
40 ,, ..	4·1 ,,
50 ,, ..	5·6 ,,
60 ,, ..	7·6 ,,
70 ,, ..	10·5 ,,
80 ,, ..	14·3 ,,
90 ,, ..	20·5 ,,

Standing quarter mile 15·8 sec.

MAXIMUM SPEEDS ON GEARS:

Gear		m.p.h.	k.p.h.
Top ..	**(mean)**	102·7	165·3
	(best)	103·6	166·8
3rd (at 6,500 r.p.m.)		84	135
2nd ,,		62	100
1st ,,		40	64

TRACTIVE EFFORT (by Tapley meter).

	Pull (lb per ton)	Equivalent gradient
Top	373	1 in 6·0
Third	535	1 in 4·2
Second	755	1 in 2·5

BRAKES (at 30 m.p.h. in neutral):

Pedal load in lb	Retardation	Equiv. stopping distance in ft.
50	0·22g	137
75	0·36g	84
100	0·45g	67
120	0·58g	52
135	0·85g	35.5

FUEL CONSUMPTION: (at steady speeds in top gear):

30 m.p.h.	40·8 m.p.g.
40 ,,	42·6 ,,
50 ,,	38·1 ,,
60 ,,	30·1 ,,
70 ,,	25·8 ,,
80 ,,	22·4 ,,
90 ,,	19·5 ,,
100 ,,	17·0 ,,

Overall fuel consumption for 1,232 miles, 22·9 m.p.g. (12·3 litres per 100 km.).
Approximate normal range 22-30 m.p.g. (12·8-9·4 litres per 100 km.).
Fuel: Super Premium grades.

TEST CONDITIONS: Weather: sunny, dry, 15-20 m.p.h. wind.
Air temperature, 49 deg. F.

STEERING: Turning circle,
Between kerbs, L, 28ft; R. 29ft.
Between walls, L. 28ft 7in.; R. 29ft 9in.
Turns of steering wheel from lock to lock, 2·75.

SPEEDOMETER CORRECTION: m.p.h.

Car speedometer ..	10	20	30	40	50	60	70	80	90	100
True speed	9	19	28	38	48	56	67	76	87	96

DATA

PRICE in component form, **£599.**
PRICE (basic), inc. close ratio gears, **£681.**
British purchase tax, **£350.**
Total (in Great Britain), **£1,031.**
Extras: Close ratio box, **£40** (fitted). Side screens, **£7 10s.** Tonneau Cover, **£5 10s.** Tachometer, **£17 10s.**

ENGINE: Capacity, 1,340 c.c. (81·78 cu. in.)
Number of cylinders, 4.
Bore and stroke, 80·96 × 65·07 mm (3·19 × 2·56in.).
Valve gear, overhead, pushrods and rockers.
Compression ratio, 9·5 to 1.
B.h.p. 85 (net) at 6,000 r.p.m. (B.h.p. per ton laden 147·8.)
M.p.h. per 1,000 r.p.m. in top gear 16·0.

WEIGHT (With 5 gal fuel): 8·6 cwt (966 lb).
Weight distribution (per cent); F, 52; R, 48.
Laden as tested, 11·6 cwt (1,302 lb).
Lb per c.c. (laden), 0·97.

BRAKES: Type, Girling drum.
Method of operation, hydraulic.
Drum dimensions: F, 8in. diameter; 1·25 in. wide R, 7in. diameter; 1·25in. wide.
Swept area: F, 63 sq. in.; R, 55 sq. in. (203 sq in. per ton laden).

TYRES: 5·20-12in.
Pressures (p.s.i.): F, 18; R, 22 (normal) F, 24; R, 28 (fast driving).

USABLE TANK CAPACITY: 5 Imperial gallons.
Oil sump, 4 pints.
Cooling system, 8 pints.

DIMENSIONS: Wheelbase, 7ft 4in.
Track: F. and R. 3ft 11in.
Length (overall), 12ft.
Width, 4ft 8in.
Height to scuttle top, 2ft 4in.
Ground clearance, 6·5in.
Frontal area, 8·5 sq. ft. (approx.).

ELECTRICAL SYSTEM: 12-volt; 38 ampère-hour battery.
Headlamps, Lucas auxiliaries.

SUSPENSION: Front, independent, coil springs and wishbones, telescopic dampers.
Rear, live axle, coil springs, located by "A" bracket, telescopic dampers.

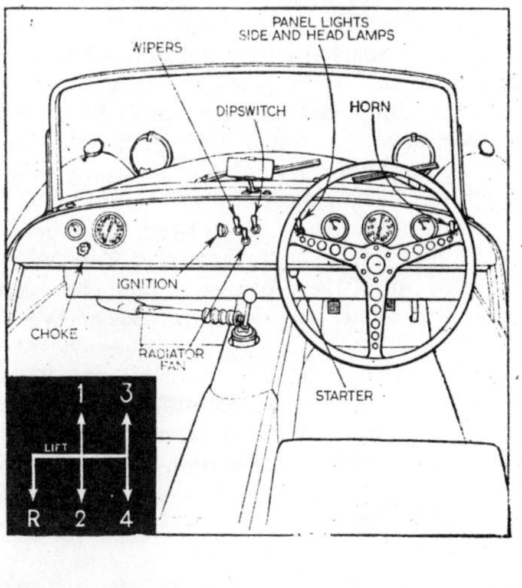

LOTUS SUPER SEVEN

Much less for the road than the track

HISTORICALLY, THE TREND in sports cars has been away from the stark, near-racing-car type of machine and toward the closed, comfortable and civilized Grand Touring car. On the whole, this is a Good Thing; it has transformed the sports car from a fussy toy into a practical piece of transportation and given it the kind of popular appeal that it otherwise could not have acquired. However, for a few this softening has removed some of the interest from the game; they would prefer the sports car to remain a racing car, with two seats (both small) and just enough lighting and muffling equipment to get the vehicle within the limits prescribed by law. For many years (too many, some say) there were no cars that met those specifications but now, in the Lotus Seven, the all-or-nothing, *pur sang,* I-*like*-rainwater-in-my-ear enthusiast can find happiness.

Our first acquaintance with the Lotus Seven came last year when we tested the Morris-engined Lotus 7-A, which had a considerable Spartan charm but only 40 bhp, and lacked the speed to match its excellent handling. Apparently this lack did not go unnoticed at home, for Lotus shortly produced a new version with a "tuned" Cosworth 109-E Ford engine and that car, the Super Seven, was, according to all reports, fast enough to satisfy almost anyone. Naturally we were eager to obtain one of these new cars for test, but expected some delay. It was a pleasant surprise, therefore, when Mr. Robert Anderson called out of the providential blue and asked if we would like to borrow his personal Super Seven. We would; and we did.

The Lotus Super Seven is in many respects exactly like the 7-A, but with some important differences—not all directly relating to the engine. It has the same frame, made up of many small round- and square-section steel tubes, and the same suspension: unequal-length A-arms in front (with the anti-roll member acting as part of the upper suspension arm) and trailing links at the rear. Transverse location of the rear axle is provided by the lower suspension member, which is a wide-based A-bracket that trails back from the chassis structure and fastens to the axle at a single point on the bottom of the drive-gear casing. This layout gives a relatively low rear roll center and little rear-axle steering. Coil springs mounted concentrically on telescopic dampers are used at each wheel. The steering is of the rack-and-pinion variety, and at 2.75 turns, lock to lock, is not unduly sensitive—although it should be noted that there is a substantial amount of lock and the steering is far from slow.

A major change in the chassis is the engine location, which is much farther forward than was the case in the 7-A. The Lotus 7-A carried 52% of its weight at the rear and in the Super Seven the engine has been located to give the car an exact 50/50 balance (all figures being with the driver in place). We must conclude that Lotus felt the car would handle better with the 50/50 weight distribution, as the engine actually had to be moved into an inconvenient location to achieve this balance. In fact, the car's fiberglass nose-piece now partially enshrouds the front of the engine, and has been made quickly removable to give access for service. We might add that the Super Seven is slightly heavier (55 lb) overall than the 7-A.

The Super Seven engine is from Ford of England's Classic, and has the same displacement but, whereas in stock form the engine develops 57 bhp (@5000 rpm), it has 90 bhp after being given the Cosworth treatment. It is widely thought that this is the same engine that Lotus is using in its Formula Junior cars, but this is not quite the case. The F-Jr engines are very highly tuned and incorporate many internal modifications to allow them to operate above 8000 rpm. In Super Seven form, a special camshaft is used and there is some reworking of the cylinder head, but that is about all that is done inside and the engine is not too reliable above 7000 rpm. Externally, there are the very impressive and effective 40-DCOE Weber carburetors and a special extractor-type exhaust system. The compression ratio is up one full number (from 8.5:1) and premium fuel is a necessity. We mention this as a point of academic interest; people who buy this car will not be of the kind who fret over the cost of fuel. In the unlikely event that there is, somewhere, a person who wants a smooth and economical Lotus Seven, the car is offered with a near-stock Ford Classic engine—having SU carburetors—at a slight reduction in cost.

With the 7-A's Morris engine, one gets the BMC series-A transmission, which can be had with a close-ratio gearset, and—logically—the 109-E engine carries with it the Ford transmission (also available with close-ratio gearing). Frankly, we were happier with the BMC transmission; the Ford unit is fine when carrying the stock power loading and pulling the stock sedan, but it shows serious signs of weakness when subjected to the Cosworth-Ford's 90 bhp. The higher loading causes a galling of the splines on which 1st gear slides, and this makes fast shifts from 1st to 2nd virtually impossible. In our test car, this misfortune occurred in the original gears and also in the replacement parts that were installed to correct the trouble, so we assume that it is not a problem peculiar to our car. Anderson plans to try a set of the optional close-ratio gears and hopes that will solve the problem—and also improve the car's acceleration, which suffers greatly under the handicap imposed by the present setup.

In making our test runs, we were unable to use 1st gear; all starts were made in 2nd. This was not as great a handicap as one might assume. The Super Seven bogs down a bit in 2nd gear, but if you catch a few thousand revolutions and bang home the clutch, it will spin its wheels enough to make a reasonably clean start. Had we used 1st gear, it would not have taken us far enough to make much difference. On the other hand, the wide spacing of the 3 speeds we used definitely slowed the acceleration. We note that in the British tests of a Super Seven equipped with close-ratio gears, standing-

A racing car—with lights and fenders.

Forward aspect with the hood removed. (The tach was out for repair.)

The test begins. Away, dull care!

LOTUS SUPER SEVEN

start ¼-mile times as low as 15.8 sec have been recorded and that seems to be a reasonable time for such a light car.

Except during the actual acceleration trials, we did not find the lack of a usable 1st gear much of a bother: even though tuned well beyond stock specifications the Super Seven's engine pulls strongly over a wide speed range and the car will perform satisfactorily when driven as though it had only 3 speeds.

Unlike the Lotus 7-A we tested last year, the Super Seven had left-hand drive, and this introduced a very interesting factor into our driving—a continuous hot-foot. The exhaust pipes are on the left, sweep next to the corner of the driver's foot-well and, as there is not the slightest trace of insulation, the heat comes right through. Also, several large gaps exist in the firewall where the steering column, etc., go through and the heat pours into the cockpit. Even though we expect a certain amount of discomfort with a machine like this, the Super Seven on several occasions gave us the distinct impression that it was really on fire. Oddly enough, the car was equipped with a heater, too; we cannot imagine to what purpose.

We suppose this, too, is "advanced thrust."

Other discomforts are created by the narrow seats, which are a press-fit for even the slight of build, and the lack of doors, which made entrance and exit with the top erected an experience that neither we, nor any onlooker, will ever forget. The problem is compounded a trifle, too, by the location of the exhaust pipe along the side of the car. This pipe curls outward at its end, and it is altogether too easy to get one's leg against the tip—another thing that left an indelible impression on at least one member of our test crew.

With all its discomforts, the Lotus Super Seven was one of the most inviting cars ever to fall into our collective hands. It is the very embodiment of that "thinly-disguised racing car" people are always talking about and, while it has serious shortcomings for day-in, day-out transportation, few cars offer as much excitement and fun. Actually, the Super Seven should be classified as a racing car, pure and simple, and the fact that it can also be driven on the street is just an incidental advantage, not its primary function. Only on a race track can the car be driven as it should be.

As a racing car, the Super Seven has considerable merit. It handles and corners like a real racing car with no modifications needed after purchase. Its fiberglass and flat-panel-aluminum body is easily repaired, and most of the pieces can be quickly stripped off for servicing. All of the mechanical elements are from low-cost, mass-produced sedans and routine maintenance should present no difficulties in either price or ease of procurement.

The one big drawback is purchase price—and even that is not as bad as it might seem. The U.S. agents for Lotus are asking $3395 POE New York for the Super Seven, and that is shockingly expensive. On the other hand, the same car may be purchased in England for slightly over $1900, and that includes the close-ratio gears. Getting the car shipped here, the duty paid, and licensed in your home state would raise the tab, naturally, but we cannot imagine how one could spend more than $2500. Still expensive, we grant you; but this is a limited-production racing car. All things considered, it is a most appealing package.

R&T

ROAD TEST

LOTUS SUPER SEVEN

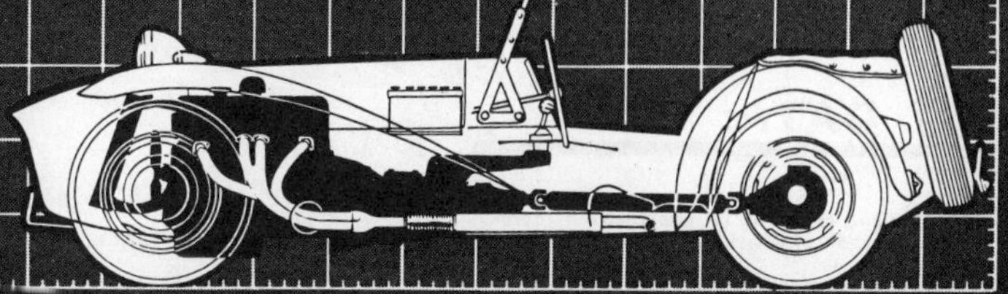

DIMENSIONS

Wheelbase, in	88.0
Tread, f and r	47.5/48.5
Over-all length, in	131.2
width	57.2
height	44.7
equivalent vol, cu ft	194
Frontal area, sq ft	14.2
Ground clearance, in	5.0
Steering ratio, o/a	n.a.
turns, lock to lock	2.7
turning circle, ft	26
Hip room, front	2 x 15.5
Hip room, rear	n.a.
Pedal to seat back, max	42.0
Floor to ground	5.0

CALCULATED DATA

Lb/hp (test wt)	14.9
Cu ft/ton mile	131.5
Mph/1000 rpm (4th)	16.1
Engine revs/mile	3720
Piston travel, ft/mile	1590
Rpm @ 2500 ft/min	5850
equivalent mph	94
R&T wear index	59.2

SPECIFICATIONS

List price, poe N.Y.	$3395
Curb weight, lb	1015
Test weight	1340
distribution, %	50/50
Tire size	5.20-13
Brake swept area	118
Engine type	4 cyl, ohv
Bore & stroke	3.19 x 2.56
Displacement, cc	1340
cu in	81.8
Compression ratio	9.5
Bhp @ rpm	90 @ 6000
equivalent mph	97
Torque, lb-ft	n.a.
equivalent mph	n.a.

GEAR RATIOS

4th (1.00)	4.11
3rd (1.41)	5.79
2nd (2.37)	9.74
1st (4.12)	16.5

SPEEDOMETER ERROR

30 mph	actual, 28.8
60 mph	58.8

PERFORMANCE

Top speed (4th), mph	102
best timed run	103
3rd (6500)	75
2nd (6500)	44
1st (6500)	26

FUEL CONSUMPTION

Normal range, mpg	19/25

ACCELERATION

0-30 mph, sec	4.0
0-40	5.2
0-50	7.4
0-60	9.9
0-70	13.1
0-80	18.1
0-100	31.0
Standing ¼ mile	16.9
speed at end	78

TAPLEY DATA

4th, lb/ton @ mph	340 @ 65
3rd	495 @ 50
2nd	off scale
Total drag at 60 mph, lb	95

ENGINE SPEED IN GEARS

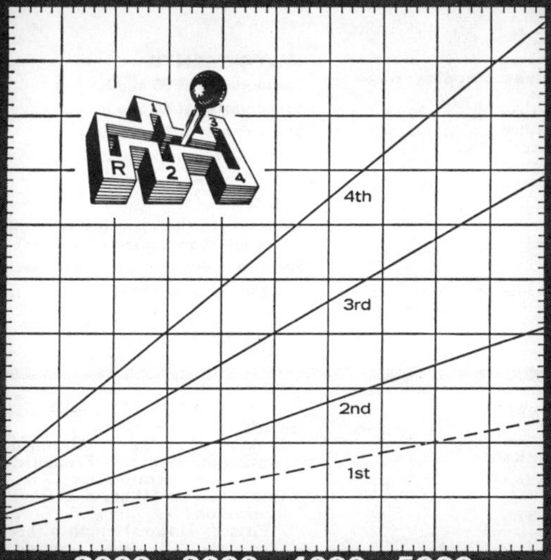

ACCELERATION & COASTING

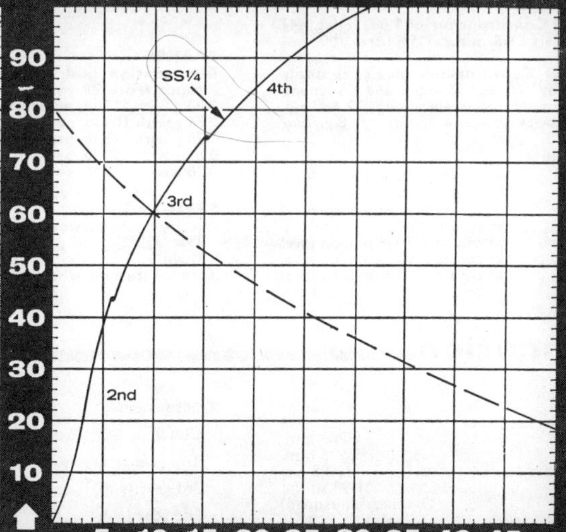

MAKE: Lotus *TYPE: Super Seven* 1500

MAKERS: Lotus Components Ltd., Delamare Road, Cheshunt, Herts.

THE Motor ROAD TEST • No. 17/63

TEST DATA:

CONDITIONS: *Weather: (Temperature 46°-54°F., Barometer 29·2-29·3 in. Hg.) Surface: Damp during most tests except acceleration and braking. Fuel: Premium grade pump petrol (98 Octane by Research Method).*

MAXIMUM SPEEDS

Flying Quarter Mile

Mean of four opposite runs	102·8 m.p.h.
Best one-way time equals	103·4 m.p.h.

"Maximile" Speed: (Timed quarter mile after one mile accelerating from rest).

Mean of four opposite runs	102·2 m.p.h.
Best one-way time equals	102·9 m.p.h.

Speed in Gears

Max. speed in 3rd gear	81·0 m.p.h.
Max. speed in 2nd gear	60·0 m.p.h.
Max. speed in 1st gear	40·0 m.p.h.

ACCELERATION TIMES From standstill

0-30 m.p.h.	2·6 sec.
0-40 m.p.h.	3·7 sec.
0-50 m.p.h.	5·7 sec.
0-60 m.p.h.	7·7 sec.
0-70 m.p.h.	10·2 sec.
0-80 m.p.h.	13·9 sec.
0-90 m.p.h.	17·7 sec.
0-100 m.p.h.	27·7 sec.
Standing quarter mile	15·9 sec.

ACCELERATION TIMES on upper ratios

	top gear	third gear
20-40 m.p.h.	6·2 sec.	3·7 sec.
30-50 m.p.h.	6·0 sec.	3·4 sec.
40-60 m.p.h.	5·5 sec.	4·1 sec.
50-70 m.p.h.	5·8 sec.	4·2 sec.
60-80 m.p.h.	6·6 sec.	5·4 sec.

HILL CLIMBING

Max. gradient climbable at steady speed

Top gear	1 in 4·7 (Tapley 460 lb./ton)
Third gear	1 in 4·3 (Tapley 510 lb./ton)
Second gear	1 in 3·0 (Tapley 705 lb./ton)

FUEL CONSUMPTION

Overall Fuel Consumption for 1,082 miles, 44¼ gallons, equals 24·8 m.p.g. (11·4 litres/100 km.)

Touring Fuel Consumption (m.p.g. at steady speed midway between 30 m.p.h. and maximum, less 5% allowance for acceleration) 22·4 m.p.g.

Fuel tank capacity (maker's figure) .. 8 gallons

Direct top gear

28½ m.p.g.	at constant 30 m.p.h. on level
28¾ m.p.g.	at constant 40 m.p.h. on level
25½ m.p.g.	at constant 50 m.p.h. on level
23½ m.p.g.	at constant 60 m.p.h. on level
23¾ m.p.g.	at constant 70 m.p.h. on level
22 m.p.g.	at constant 80 m.p.h. on level
18½ m.p.g.	at constant 90 m.p.h. on level

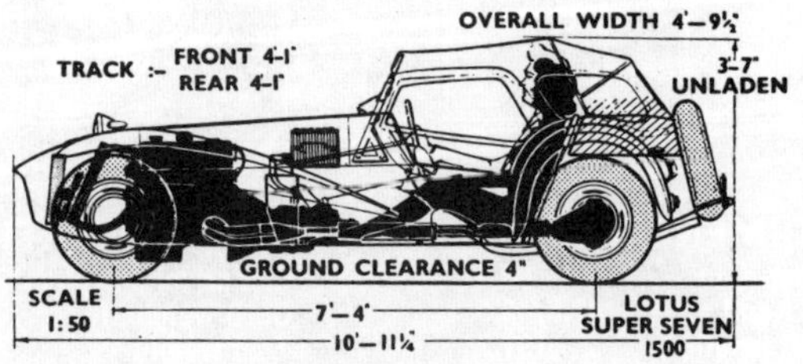

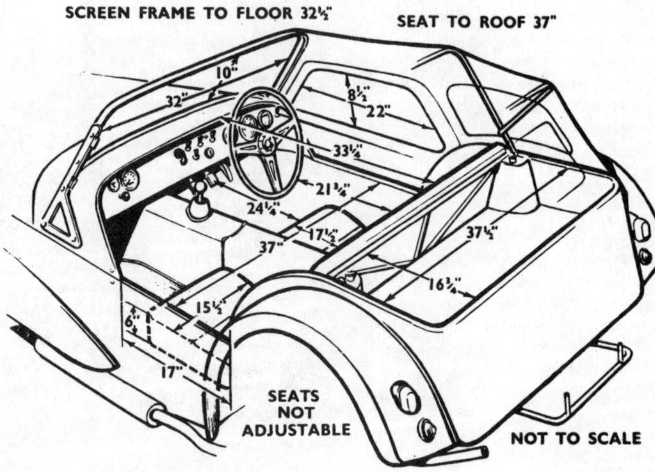

BRAKES

Deceleration and equivalent stopping distance from 30 m.p.h.

1·00 g with 115 lb. pedal pressure	(30 ft.)
0·94 g with 105 lb. pedal pressure	(23 ft.)
0·70 g with 75 lb. pedal pressure	(42¾ ft.)
0.61 g with 50 lb. pedal pressure	(49¼ ft.)
0·28 g with 25 lb. pedal pressure	(107 ft.)

STEERING

Turning circle between kerbs:

Left	25¾ ft.
Right	26½ ft.
Turns of steering wheel from lock to lock	2¾

INSTRUMENTS

Speedometer at 30 m.p.h.	9% fast
Speedometer at 60 m.p.h.	accurate
Speedometer at 90 m.p.h.	1% fast
Distance recorder	accurate

WEIGHT

Kerb weight (unladen, but with oil, coolant and fuel for approximately 50 miles)	9½ cwt.
Front/rear distribution of kerb weight	55/45
Weight laden as tested	12½ cwt.

Specification

Engine

Cylinders	4
Bore	80·63 mm.
Stroke	72·75 mm.
Cubic capacity	1,498 c.c.
Piston area	31·92 sq. in.
Valves	Overhead (pushrod)
Compression ratio	9·5/1
Carburetters	Two 40 DCOE Webers
Fuel pump	AC Mechanical
Ignition timing control	Centrifugal
Oil filter	Full flow
Maximum power (gross)	95 b.h.p.
at	6,000 r.p.m.
Maximum torque (gross)	95 lb. ft.
at	4,500 r.p.m.
Piston speed at maximum b.h.p.	2,870 ft./min.

Transmission

Clutch	8 in. Borg & Beck s.d.p.
Top gear (s/m)	4·1
3rd gear (s/m)	5·79
2nd gear (s/m)	6·98
1st gear (s/m)	10·31
Propeller shaft	B.R.D. open
Final drive	Hypoid bevel
Top gear m.p.h. at 1,000 r.p.m.	15·3
Top gear m.p.h. at 1,000 ft./min. piston speed	31·9

Chassis

Brakes:	Girling disc and drum
Brake dimensions:	Front discs: 9½ in. dia. Rear drums: 7 in. × 1¼ in. wide
Friction areas:	44¼ sq. in. of friction lining area
Suspension:	
Front:	Unequal length wishbones with coil spring damper units
Rear:	A-bracket with parallel radius arms and coil spring damper units
Shock absorbers:	
Front / Rear	Armstrong telescopic
Steering gear:	Alford and Alder rack and pinion
Tyres:	4·50—13 Dunlop C41 or India C.46 Autoway

Lotus Super Seven (1500)

AS a tool for satisfying the "racer" in most of us, the Lotus Super Seven is an unqualified success. It does it at such a low price as to be remarkable and it would be unreasonable to expect very much comfort or refinement. There is plenty of performance and good road-holding but except for the arch-enthusiast, it would not be acceptable for everyday transport. As in most Lotuses up to the monocoque 25 Grand Prix racing car, the basis of the Super Seven is an extremely light tubular structure, and with the five-bearing 1½-litre Ford Classic engine tuned to produce 95 b.h.p., it has a power to weight ratio close to 200 b.h.p. per ton. Consequently, acceleration is very fierce indeed; the equal of almost any other vehicle on the road. Disc brakes match the performance and good handling complements it so far as smooth roads go. The ride is stiff and uncomfortable at low speeds and weather equipment, although an improvement over previous Sevens, remains rather sketchy. Cockpit space and luggage room are restricted, emphasizing that the Lotus is intended for the enthusiast to whom low-cost performance is worth extreme sacrifices. More specifically, it is aimed at the enthusiast with the ability and time to assemble his own car and save the purchase tax on works-completed vehicles.

Spare-looking (*top*) the Lotus bonnet is only a little over knee high. The oil cooler and electric cooling fan can be seen through the front grille. (*Below*) The small wood-rimmed steering wheel and the low build of the car encourage a reclining, long-arm driving position. The speedometer, of secondary importance to the tachometer, is placed in front of the passenger.

Acceleration

THE bite of the Lotus is even worse (or better according to how one looks at it) than its bark which is considerable. The exhaust is full-throated and loud; definitely not for the town, where it could give serious offence, but a delight to the enthusiast

In Brief

Price (without the extras mentioned in text) £695 plus purchase tax £173 15s. equals £868 15s. Price in kit form (without extras) £645.

Capacity	1,498 c.c.
Unladen kerb weight	9½ cwt.
Acceleration:	
20-40 m.p.h. in top gear	6.2 sec.
0-50 m.p.h. through gears	5.7 sec.
Maximum top gear gradient	1 in 4.7
Maximum speed	102.8 m.p.h.
Overall fuel consumption	24.8 m.p.g.
Touring fuel consumption	22.4 m.p.g.
Gearing:	15.3 m.p.h. in top gear at 1,000 r.p.m.

Lotus Super Seven

Without the sidescreens shown here (*top*) the Lotus has an almost fragile appearance. The stoneguards at the front of the rear wings are a practical innovation. (*Left*) The hood frame folds up and the fabric buttons on with press studs all round. The hood will stow in the space behind the seats which is also the only possible luggage accommodation. A neat tonneau cover may be supplied. (*Below*) The Cosworth-modified five-bearing Ford Classic engine. The dipstick is hard to get at under the plastic nose cowl ahead of the front carburetter. Rubber hoses alongside the engine lead to the test car's heater at the top of the picture.

in the right place. The sharp crackle is more than mere noise however. It is the voice of a Cosworth Ford with two double-choke Weber 40 DCOE carburetters, modified manifolds, cylinder head, and non-standard camshaft. At 6,000 r.p.m. it is producing 95 b.h.p. and over-enthusiasm from a standing start can leave long black lines of tyre tread on dry concrete. 50 m.p.h. can be reached in under 6 seconds and the quarter-mile mark passed in less than 16. The Lotus is one of the few cars which will accelerate to 100 m.p.h. and brake to a stop again in a time approaching the half minute, and it is almost certainly the cheapest production car ever to approach this. The maximum speed of nearly 103 m.p.h. was achieved at around 6,400 r.p.m. and the engine was taken to 6,500 in the indirect gears during the performance tests and on the road quite frequently without any apparent ill effects.

The smoothness of the five-bearing crankshaft makes the new engine a suitable choice and although there is no red line on the tachometer it appeared capable of revving higher if there had been any need. There is a good deal of mechanical clatter as well as hoarse sucking noises from the Webers to a listener standing at the front of the car, but inside this is all drowned by the exhaust. Idling is uneven and seemed to vary between 900 r.p.m. and about 1,800 r.p.m. with very richly set carburetters which were responsible for the heavy low-speed fuel consumption. The choke was never found necessary even after the car had been left standing out all night but care had to be taken with the throttle when starting the engine hot in case sudden floods of neat petrol drowned the plugs. This was really the only trace of temperament the engine had, although, not surprisingly, the power only starts asserting itself above 2,000 r.p.m.

Cooling is by the draught through the radiator when the car is moving, assisted by an electric fan which is switched on in traffic. This was seldom found necessary; in fact the temperature remained under 80°C. during all normal running (away from slowly shuffling traffic) one day when the outside temperature hovered round 50°F. (10°C.). During the test, this fan became inoperative and it was occasionally necessary to bring the interior heater blower into service in its place. This, together with the warm air which blows in from the engine compartment at speeds over 50 m.p.h. could make the interior uncomfortably hot. The oil cooler with which the test car was equipped is an optional extra at £15.

Close ratio gears

THE competition clutch was so heavy as to be difficult to operate at all, and the pedal uncomfortably angled which made traffic driving most unpleasant. For fast gearchanges however, it is much more suitable and has a short travel. The gear lever is stumpy and needs a quick, firm movement with care for going from first to second owing to the weakness of the reverse stop; otherwise, the changes are clean. The test car was supplied with the close-ratio box which costs an extra £40, gave splendid fast changes and seemed worthwhile to allow the engine to give its best. The standing-starts proved too much for first gear however, which failed during the test.

Like the clutch, the brakes need a firm pressure. They are Girling discs on the front with drum rears and while extremely resistant to fade, they were sometimes a little uneven when stopping from high speeds. The handbrake above the passenger's knees worked on a 1 in 3 test hill but it is extremely difficult to operate. The light steering has very little self-centring action and feels rather dead, although there is some kick-back on bumps. High speed stability is impaired by this and by engine torque reaction which can deflect the car off course when the throttle is opened or closed.

Cornering on smooth roads, the Lotus behaves in an exemplary fashion. There is a pleasant understeer and at speed the car behaves precisely as directed with a mild breakaway at the rear. In the wet, discretion is called for with the throttle, especially in the lower gears and the steering is very high geared making over-correction of slides rather easy for the unpractised. Smooth roads in the dry however, are sheer joy and fast, open, main road bends can be negotiated on "lines" in the prescribed manner with scarcely any body roll.

On rough surfaces, the firmness of the damping gives a bumpy ride and the rigid back axle shows itself to be rather unruly. The tubular chassis frame whips, giving a good deal of scuttle shake, making the front wings and headlamps vibrate rather alarmingly. The springs have a good deal of movement, demonstrated when the back tyres scuffed the inside of the rear wings with the increased *g* force on the M.I.R.A. bankings but they hardly budged over small bumps. Main road undulations are coped with well at speed but potholes cause some discomfort and can upset the car's stability on a corner.

The much improved hood gives the Lotus a slightly dragster look. There was little ground clearance for the exhaust system which now comes out at the back instead of the side.

Sacrifices

HAVING dwelt at some length on the fine performance, and the exhilaration of driving this splendid and truly sporting car, stock must be taken of the drawbacks of owning one. The driving position gives a clue to what conditions must be like in the cockpit of a current Formula Junior or Grand Prix racing car. It is small and cramped, with a diminutive 15-inch steering wheel at arms' length and the elbows overhang the driving seat, the left resting on the transmission tunnel and the right over-hanging the frame tube at the side of the car. Non-adjustable seats demand a semi-reclining position fitting different heights of driver remarkably well; heavy coats, however, are difficult to accommodate, and so are large-sized shoes on the narrow toe-board.

The wood-rimmed steering wheel is quite comfortable although most drivers would prefer a thicker rim. Instruments are limited to a tachometer, oil pressure gauge, and water thermometer in front of the driver and a speedometer and ammeter on the passenger's side. A fuel gauge seems a curious omission.

Weather protection is a great improvement on earlier Super Sevens and sidescreens are now available. New transparent panels in the hood make the car much easier to see out of, and with the hood and sidescreens in position the interior is really quite cosy, if not very draught or waterproof. A good way of motoring the Lotus is solo with a tonneau cover over the passenger's seat and a segment filling the cutaway by the driver's right elbow. The flared glass-fibre wings deflect most of the spray from a wet road but the hot exhaust pipe is very close to the legs of passengers getting in or out. Space behind the seats will hold the hood when the tonneau is in place, or the tonneau when the hood is up, but proves a little small for the sidescreen frames. The inside fuel filler is reached by unbuttoning a corner of the hood so that luggage in the rear well may get splashed with petrol.

Climatic

OUR affection for the Lotus Super Seven quite literally would change with the weather. On a good day, driving it over open main roads without the hood was thrilling, but in hot damp traffic the heavy clutch and the drips and the draughts made it miserable. Depending on one's acceptance or rejection of its discomforts and starkness, the Lotus will be accepted or rejected. Its suitability for club racing, sprints, or driving tests is obvious although it might prove a fragile rally car. It is quite outstanding for low-cost, high-performance sporting motoring.

Coachwork and Equipment

Starting handle	None
Battery mounting	Under bonnet
Jack	None
Jacking points	Any convenient point on chassis
Standard tool kit	None
Exterior lights: 2 side, 2 rear, 2 head, stop and number plate.	
Number of electrical fuses	2
Direction indicators	Self cancelling flashers extra
Windscreen wipers	Two-blade, electric, self-cancelling
Windscreen washers	None
Sun visors	None
Instruments: Speedometer with total mileage recorder, oil pressure, water temperature, ammeter.	
Warning lights	None
Locks:	
With ignition key	Ignition
With other keys	None
Glove lockers	None
Map pockets	None
Parcel shelves	None
Ashtrays	None
Cigar lighters	None
Interior lights	None
Interior heater	Optional extra
Car radio	None
Extras available: Sidescreens, heater, tonneau cover, flashing indicators, tachometer.	
Upholstery material	Vynide
Floor covering	Rubber mats
Exterior colours standardized: Any colour at extra cost.	
Alternative body styles	None

Maintenance

Sump	4 pints, S.A.E. 40/50
Gearbox	1¾ pints, S.A.E. 80 EP
Rear axle	1¾ pints, S.A.E. 80 EP
Steering gear lubricant	Multi-purpose grease
Cooling system capacity	8 pints (2 drain taps)
Chassis lubrication	None
Ignition timing	3° before t.d.c. static
Contact breaker gap	0.014-0.016 in.
Sparking plug type	Champion N5
Sparking plug gap	0.025 in.
Valve timing: Inlet opens 40° b.t.d.c. and closes 76° a.b.d.c. Exhaust opens 76° b.b.d.c. and closes 40° a.t.d.c.	
Tappet clearances: (cold)	inlet 0.017 in. exhaust 0.020 in.
Front wheel toe-in	⅛ in.
Camber angle	1° positive
Castor angle	5°
Steering swivel pin inclination	9°
Tyre pressures:	
Front	22 lb.
Rear	22 lb.
Brake fluid	Girling
Battery type and capacity	12 volt, 38 amp.-hr.
Miscellaneous: Trunnion to vertical link bearings requires filling with oil.	

To the enthusiast the Lotus Seven means handling, austerity and a harshness associated with square-rigger sports cars.

CHRIS BECK ROAD TESTS . . .

THE SIMPLICITY SEVEN

SINCE its introduction at the Earls Court Motor Show in 1957, Colin Chapman's stark Lotus Seven has proved his most popular and successful production creation in 15 years.

Aimed at the enthusiast, its main claims to fame were the remarkable roadholding capabilities which were to become world famous.

The sporting fraternity was divided in its opinions as to whether the machine would sell. Some said it was far too basic, austere and fragile and would never stand up to everyday hack use, but the opposition claimed that its handling, roadholding and simplicity would appeal to the sporting purist, and these features would far outweigh the deficiencies.

Hundreds of these little lightweights have been produced at the Cheshunt factory since then and have found their way into the hearts of enthusiasts all over the globe. In many ways its lack of chrome-plate, thinly padded seats, draughty cockpit and flimsy-looking classic-line bodywork has been quite a sales gimmick. A substantial percentage of the cars are sold in the US, where motorists regard luxury and comfort in an automobile as a primary necessity. This market dispells any theories held by pessimists as to the car's austerity.

The foundation of this model was laid down in 1953 when the first Mark Six Lotuses were built purely for competition. When production of these stopped in 1955 Chapman said the Seven would be an improved road version of the Six. It was not until 1957 that work really began in earnest on the car as the factory had too many competition car commitments beforehand.

In competition, the Seven and its bigger-engined brother, the Super Seven, have won acclaim in sports car racing on circuits in all parts of the world, from Laguna Seca, California, to Sandown Park, Victoria.

Oddly enough SPORTS CAR WORLD has never tested a completely standard Lotus Seven. Since previous tests on Sevens have been on racing models or Supers, it was decided to find and test one. It is the cheapest Lotus available in Australia, selling for a shade under £1200.

Sydney motor sport enthusiast and avid Lotus owner Bob Black was approached and asked if his car could be used for the test. He agreed willingly as he also wanted to know what the car could do under this treatment.

Black's car, finished in a lustrous flame orange, is vastly different from the standard Sevens shown at the London Salon in 1957 even though it is still completely "as from the factory". When the model was introduced it was powered by a sidevalve Ford 10 motor, had cycle guards, a three speed gear box and a rudely austere interior when compared with today's product.

In its five years of production the car has been re-engined, had its frame and bodywork refined and fitted with a four speed gearbox. Lotus makes very few completely standard Sevens — most of them are fitted with some sort of optional engine or gearbox. In the United States a special standard model called the Seven A is sold. This car is fitted with 1098 cc Austin Healey Sprite engine to make the spare parts situation easier for owners. Of course, the extra power and torque available from the BMC A-series motor makes it a much faster and more accelerative vehicle than the English model, which is equipped with a 997 cc Anglia with twin 1.25 in SU carburettors.

As we said earlier, Black's car is a perfectly standard Anglia-powered Seven and so far the motor has not been altered from factory specifications. Lotus leaves the head, block, crankshaft, exhaust manifold and ignition the same as on an ordinary Anglia. The horsepower-soaking fan is removed and the large slanted radiator is supposed to be able to cope with the cooling. Bob found, soon after he bought the car, that in traffic it overheated very quickly and so he fitted an electric fan which does a remarkable job.

The engine compartment is simple and all parts of the motor are readily accessible. Installed on the engine bulkhead are the battery, clutch and brake master cylinders and the voltage regulator.

A standard Anglia gearbox with a Triumph Herald remote shift mechanism protrudes back into the cockpit and the gear lever is just four

Handling and roadholding are its two finest features. Bends can be taken at seemingly suicidal speeds.

The standard oversquare Anglia motor, fitted with twin 1.25 inch SUs, develops 45 bhp at 5500 rpm.

Austerity is the password to the cockpit. With the hood down at high speed, it is amazingly quiet.

From this angle, the car looks like a crab's claw. Styling is along the traditional lines.

Spare wheel is carried on the number-plate bracket at the rear. Tail-lights are mounted on mudguards.

inches long and topped by a comfortable white plastic ball-knob.

Designed with the enthusiast in mind, the Seven lacks those creature comforts considered essential by many present day sports car owners. For instance, there are no doors, so it's not the type of carriage in which to take a girl to a ball. The aluminium driveshaft tunnel sticks up almost a foot from the floor and from it pokes the gear lever.

Seats are part of the bodywork and are non-adjustable, but there is ample leg room. Red vinyl covers the long thin aluminium dash which has an ammeter on the left-hand side, an oil pressure gauge, a 130 mph speedometer and a temperature gauge on the right, in front of the driver. In the centre, there is an assortment of toggle switches and a key ignition.

Slipping into the thinly, padded seats the driver's hand seems to fall upon the small, frail-looking wood-rimmed steering wheel with a plastic Lotus boss in the centre. There is a closeness to mother earth only associated with a few of today's sport cars. You sit low in the car and your legs just touch the pedals.

Behind the occupants, in the short stubby tail, there is a five gallon fuel tank and above it a small parcel tray which will only carry the tonneau and the hood. As far as luggage space is concerned there is none; this is not really the car for a long Interstate trip. At the rear of the car there is a combination spare wheel and number plate bracket, similar to the T-series MGs.

Front suspension is independent by wishbones and coil springs — most of the unit is from a Triumph Herald, but the lower wishbone is Lotus. Extremely well located, the Standard 10 live rear axle is suspended by leading arms, coil springs and Panhard rods. Telescopic dampers are used throughout.

Only a slight jab at the starter button is needed to send the motor coughing into life. After a brief warming up period it runs quite smoothly and the oversquare motor revs through the range quickly. During our acceleration runs, with two 13 stoners aboard, the little car found no trouble in spinning its wheels in first gear and chirp could be produced in second gear. Of course, the secret is that the motor, which produces 45 bhp at 6000 rpm, only has eight cwt to push along. This is just on four cwt lighter than a Mk2A Sprite which has 55 bhp on tap.

Badly spaced gearbox ratios did not show the car up at its best. Exactly the same as in the standard Anglia, we found that both first and second were far too slow by modern sports car standards and it's our opinion that the car could be greatly improved by a gearbox that would give 32 mph in first cog and 54 in second In its present form 25 is available in first and the valves begin to complain around 42 mph in second. Third is very versatile and runs to 73 mph, but there is far too wide a gap between it and second and this is troublesome when going hard through 40 to 55 mph corners — the pick-up is not really good. Maximum in fourth gear was 82 mph, but the engine does not strain to attain it, and on good hot-mix roads one feels this speed could be maintained all day.

The thin tube Brooklands-type silencer runs along the passenger's side of the car after coming out through the underside of the front left-

PERFORMANCE

Top speed average		81 mph
Fastest run		83 mph
Maximum, first		25 mph
Maximum, second		42 mph
Maximum, third		73 mph
Maximum, fourth		83 mph
Standing quarter mile average		20.15 seconds
Fastest run		19.8 seconds
0 to 30 mph		4.2 seconds
0 to 40 mph		6.7 seconds
0 to 50 mph		10.2 seconds
0 to 60 mph		14.8 seconds
0 to 70 mph		21.7 seconds
0 to 80 mph		35.1 seconds
	TOP	THIRD
40 to 60 mph	11.1 seconds	7.2 seconds
50 to 70 mph	13.6 seconds	13.5 seconds
60 to 80 mph	21 seconds	NA
Brake fade resistance on test hill		88 percent
Fuel Consumption, overall		35 mpg
Fuel Consumption, cruising		38 mpg

With the hood up the Seven is rather a spacious little sports car, although it flaps at high speed.

hand mudguard. Its note is raspy, but was not obtrusive and even at top speed, with the hood down, normal conversation could be carried on quite easily.

Like most sports cars the wind problem is ever present, although it is not unduly annoying. Anyway, what is a sports car without wind whipping around one's gills?

Ride is decidedly choppy over rough surfaces and if taken on to dirt roads of the type commonly seen in this country, its protestations are numerous. Even on tar-aggregate roads it vibrates like a body-conditioner and steering is best done by holding one hand around the bottom spoke of the alloy-wood steering wheel.

It revels on hot-mix and on this type of surface its amazing road-holding, for which it is world renowned, comes to light. It corners so well that one feels it must use independent suspension on the rear. Corners can be taken at almost suicidal speeds with the car slightly drifting, but it never does anything spectacular. When cornering on the limit we found it hard to assess whether it oversteered, understeered or what. Initially it understeers slightly and then it gradually goes back to a neutral attitude. Wherever you point the steering wheel it goes. If the accelerator is used carefully oversteer can be induced, but only in a small way.

Body roll is negligible. Even the most inexperienced driver could have a ball in this car and not get into any serious trouble unless he did something completely stupid.

It is a true sports car, the main appeal of which lies in its austerity and roadholding. It will not appeal to the person who wants the comforts and luxuries of an MGB or TR4, but I feel it is the type of car I would like to own to take out in the dawn hours on a Sunday morning. It is the ideal car for those who have a sedan as well because frankly, this is not everyday, utilitarian transport. #

SPECIFICATIONS

CHASSIS AND BODY DIMENSIONS:

Wheelbase	7 ft 4 in
Track, front	3 ft 11 in
Track, rear	3 ft 11 in
Ground Clearance	$6\frac{1}{2}$ in
Turning circle	30 ft 0 in
Turns, lock to lock	2.25
Overall length	12 ft 0 in
Overall width	4 ft 8 in
Overall height	2 ft 4 in

CHASSIS:

Steering type	rack and pinion
Brake type	drums all round
Suspension, front	independent wishbones and coils
Suspension, rear	live axle, leading arms, coil springs and Panhard rod.
Shock absorbers	telescopic
Tyre size	5.20 x 13

Weight	$8\frac{1}{2}$ cwt
Fuel tank capacity	5.25 gals
Approx cruising range	200 miles

ENGINE:

Cylinders	four in line
Bore and stroke	80.9 mm by 48.4 mm
Cubic capacity	997 cc
Compression ratio	8.9 to 1
Fuel requirement	95 octane
Valves	pushrod overhead
Maximum power	45 bhp at 5000 rpm
Maximum torque	53 ft/lbs at 2700 rpm

TRANSMISSION:

Overall ratios

First	16.9
Second (synchro)	9.8
Third (synchro)	5.8
Fourth (synchro)	4.1
Final drive	4.87 to 1

SUPER SEVEN

Fast four-wheeled motorcycle

MANY people's introduction to Lotus motoring, if not their sports car baptism, is the Lotus 7. Many argue as to the precise definition of a sports car, but no one could doubt for a moment that, whatever a sports car may be, the Lotus 7—simple, light, sparse, noisy and raceable—is one.

Colin Chapman always intended to make a successor to the Mk 6, a simple spaceframe car with proprietary coil/wishbone front suspension and rigid rear axle, alloy panel bodywork and cycle-type wings, which would be an inexpensive road and track device. The car eventually appeared at the 1957 Earls Court show, fitted with the faithful sidevalve 1172 Ford unit; later the BMC A-series unit and 1100 Climax motors were used, and the car became a familiar sight in club racing.

In 1960 the Series 2 version made its bow, with 13-ins instead of 15-ins wheels, fibreglass nose cowl and wings, and a refined spaceframe using a Standard-Triumph rather than a BMC rear axle, still with coils and trailing arms but adopting a triangulated A-bracket. Price with standard 105E engine was £499, and naturally the car sold very well; it is still very much in production, although none were made for almost 12 months following the factory move from Cheshunt to Norfolk. Roughly 2500 have been sold in this country alone, and they continue to find a ready market.

When we visited the Lotus factory no driveable 7 was on hand for us to try, although a batch of very pretty Super 7s with full trim, Elan wheels (which are now a standard fitting) and roll-over bars were awaiting despatch to Canada. So to remind myself what Lotus 7 motoring was like I visited Caterham Car Sales, in Caterham, Surrey, who are the only Lotus dealers specializing exclusively in 7s. Bossman Graham Nearn has been selling them since the Series 1 days in 1959, and finds them as popular as ever—he has sold 25 new kits since the October show—and at the time of our visit there were a dozen second-hand 7s in stock.

The car I borrowed was an immaculate yellow example belonging to Melvyn White, and its condition belied the fact that it was two years old and had done 32,000 miles. There is no doubt that a Lotus 7, properly looked after, can survive 16,000 hard road miles a year without any trouble. This was the Super 7 model, with 95 bhp Cosworth-tweaked 1500 Ford motor and twin Webers, plus standard ratio box and effective weather equipment—standard wear for current models is the 1500 GT Cortina engine with single twin-choke Weber and Lotus manifolding, and in kit form the car costs £645.

"My" car boasted a nicely carpeted interior and, on a rather drizzly afternoon, was quite snug once in motion with the hood down and sidescreens in position. Seats, wheel and pedal are all non-adjustable, but the arm's-length driving position felt very comfortable for my 5 ft 10 ins, and the average bottom fits comfortably between the propshaft tunnel and the body sides on the simple Vynide seat cushion.

Dash layout is a matter for the builder's personal preference, but holes are drilled for rev-counter and oil and water gauges ahead of the driver, with the speedo and ammeter in front of the passenger. Starting involves a fair amount of groping around the bulkhead, where the starter button (direct onto the solenoid) and the awkward sideways mounted handbrake live, but the little gearlever is perfectly positioned. Very fast changes from first to second and from third to top can be made with the hand in a thumbs-up gesture, the thumb pivoting the hand against the dashboard and one's fist grabbing the lever back the two inches required to find the next cog.

As the afternoon was drizzly the roads were quite slippery, and enormous fun could be had flinging the Lotus into tight bends and kicking the back round under power to produce an ego-boosting opposite-lock slide. At higher speeds the car demanded much more respect, and taking a long series of curves at 90 mph required a steady hand and a light touch on the wheel; the back wheels were likely to hop about a little on bumps, which felt slightly disconcerting. But always the car remains very controllable; its small size and very direct steering help to make it feel precise and taut.

The Lotus 7's great virtue is the way it deals with other road users, making it a great frustration-eraser on crowded roads. It is very small and very accelerative; when a gap appears in the traffic it darts through it in a very satisfying way, and although wheelspin is a very real problem with so much power in a light rigid axle car, the car rockets forward in almost any gear.

Road test figures of the 1500 Super 7 give 0-60 in 6.8 secs and a 15.4 secs standing quarter mile, and though the car I drove did not have close ratio gears, its "dartability"—the combination of Mini-like manoeuvrability and low-speed get-away—made it unbeatable on crowded roads, certainly up to Mrs Castle's limit. The close ratio gears cost £50 extra, but eliminate the wide gap between second and third, at the expense of losing the very close gap between first and second, which sounds marvellous in a flat-out standing start—the revs hardly fall as one snatches second gear.

Maximum speed is not astronomical, thanks to low gearing (4.1 to 1) and the uncompromisingly unaerodynamic flat screen and wings, but is certainly over 100 mph, and the car rushed up to 95 with never a pause for breath. The disc front/drum rear braking system has only 9 cwt to deal with and is very effective.

How practical is the Lotus 7 as a road car? The weather equipment nowadays is very snug, and though there are no doors, the sidescreens hinge about the windscreen and make it all very cosy. However, long distances with the hood up tend to be tiresome for two reasons: the fuel filler cap, just behind the passenger and inside the hood when it is up, can give off fumes to sensitive nostrils; and the car's thunderously noisy exhaust system becomes even more evident with the hood up. There are beautifully equipped *Gran Turismo* (in the original sense) Lotus 7s about with full upholstery and radio, and no doubt these owners have rerouted the fuel filler and fitted more elaborate exhaust systems than the standard setup, which sings its song a few inches below the passenger's left ear. Other sacrifices are few: there is no fuel gauge, but the experienced Lotuseer carries a graduated stick to pop in the tank and take a reading. The suspension is hard, but the overcoat that is *de rigeur* to keep out the elements when one drives a 7 helps to insulate the bumps.

Somebody once described the Lotus 7 as a four-wheeled motorcycle, and I know just what he meant. To own one as your sole form of transport you must be young, hardy, a little deaf and have an understanding girl-friend or a good mackintosh; but as occasional transport when the sun shines and the cobwebs need blowing away, it is hard to beat.

LOTUSES I HAVE KNOWN

David Phipps (who used to work there) reminisces

THE FIRST LOTUS I EVER drove was a Seven with a side valve Ford engine—the original Lotus Seven, in fact. I collected it from Hornsey at 8.30 on a cold November evening after waiting three hours while Colin Chapman and Mike Costin finished building it. In view of the weather my wife decided it would be nice to have the hood up, but after we had put it up I found I couldn't get in—so I got in first and the hood was fastened around me.

Even with the hood up it was still pretty draughty as we trickled out

along A10, taking more care than usual not to exceed 50 in the 40 areas. 'Isn't it wonderful' I shouted 'to be driving a Lotus at last?' 'No' my wife bawled, huddling further down into the foot well. 'I would rather be in the Morris Eight . . .' (A 1937 Morris was our normal means of transport at this time.)

We had just got out into the country when suddenly everything became ominously quiet and we coasted to a halt. The engineer in me soon detected that something was wrong, and after staring gloomily under the bonnet I searched along the roadside for a stick to dip the petrol tank. Sure enough it came out bone dry and I concluded we were out of petrol—late at night and miles from anywhere. There was no fuel gauge, of course, and we were accustomed to full tanks on road test cars.

Having filled the tank we got to Norfolk without any further problems, finding that the little car would do its maximum 80mph round most of the corners as well as along the straights, but next morning a major snag arose when we went to show it to some local enthusiasts and found we had a puncture. It looked a very simple task to change the wheel, but inspection revealed that there was no jack—and no air in the spare tyre.

For the rest of the weekend the sun shone and we had a really marvellous time haring around the country lanes and generally alarming the staid Norfolk populace. A neighbouring farmer predicted an untimely end for us due to the low build of the car, but we managed to avoid getting under any trucks or tractors and set out for the return journey to London in high spirits.

The next Seven which came my way had a Climax engine and racing

tyres, and I used it for a trip to the Cranleigh School where I was giving a talk to the motor club about sports cars. Once again it was midwinter, and in view of my earlier experience with the hood I left it down altogether, relying on numerous layers of clothing to keep me warm. On the way home I came across several ice patches, and the combination of the Climax engine and racing tyres made them interesting to say the least.

My next Seven had a 1500cc Cosworth Ford engine and really went like the clappers. I drove it for the first time at a Brands Hatch press day, and was told that the rev limit was 6000. Going up to Hawthorn Bend for the first time I glanced down at the rev counter and saw it was reading 7000 in top, so I concluded that Mike Costin was being unduly cautious. Subsequently I used the car for another trip to Norfolk, this time to the school where I used to teach, and while I was having sherry in the headmaster's study a group of boys carried it away and hid it under a hedge; the next time I went there I used a Mark IX Jaguar.

In the summer of 1958 I drove a Lotus Elite for the first time on a short triangular road course starting and finishing at Michael Christie's Alexander Engineering works. At this time Michael Christie was British concessionaire for the Elite, and he talked enthusiastically about a trip through Germany in one with the Duke of Kent. I was able to do a continental journey in an Elite myself the following spring, when I took the one and only demonstration model to the Geneva show. Of course, the show had been open almost a week before the car was ready and it was still being worked on when I went to collect it. When I finally managed to get my hands on it I was absolutely delighted with the thing, the only snag being that the engine mounting rubbers were rather too soft and the engine didn't like being driven at anything other than full throttle. Needless to say the vibration at tickover contrived to loosen a carburettor union, and I was only a few miles into France, with the fuel gauge firmly stuck at full when once more I found myself gliding silently to a halt.

I repeated the journey to Geneva two years later in a Series Two Elite, and this time I had no problems whatsoever. The car was also much quieter, and ran straighter thanks to its improved rear suspension; the aerodynamics showed up to good effect, too, when I drove through a heavy snowstorm without needing to use the screen wipers. By this time the Elite had become an ideal car for continental touring, with a very moderate fuel consumption, adequate luggage capacity, high cruising speed and marvellous handling and brakes.

Soon after I drove my first Elite I had my first taste of single-seater motoring in a Formula Junior Lotus 18. By today's standards the 18 was a very basic car with incredibly narrow tyres, but at that time it seemed just about the ultimate in cornering power. I had driven quite a lot of so-called sports cars round Goodwood, but from the seat of a Lotus 18 the circuit took on a completely new character; I had never seen Chichester cathedral spire leaning so much before.

The following year it leaned even more when I drove a Lotus 20, and having become a little braver in the interim I decided I could use full throttle in second coming out of the chicane. Yet I only spun once.

The chief trouble with modern single-seaters is that they are not made for normal people—only for midgets of 5ft 8 to 5ft 10. To get my 6ft 8in into the 20 I had to take the seat out, and even after I had done that I still stuck out at least a foot—which must have had a dreadful effect on the car's maximum speed. I also had to take my shoes off to avoid pressing all three pedals at once. However, I did manage to go quickly enough to get a feeling of what it was all about, and to convince myself that I would never make a racing driver. In the 18 I had done three laps on as many

1 *The remarkable Seven, still one of the quickest British cars;* **2** *The 20, Phipps up (frontal area?);* **3** *The Elite, of fond memory*

cylinders before I realised why everyone was waving plug spanners at me, and in the 20 I kept on arriving at corners in the wrong gear (or no gear at all), due to the general sloppiness of the gearshift.

During the summer of 1959 I set out on a road test of the Team Lotus 17 complete with stage three Coventry Climax engine, but the combined weight of driver and 'riding mechanic' proved too much for the differential mountings and we returned to the factory at the end of a tow rope having been rescued from darkest Cambridgeshire by Colin Chapman and Mike Costin.

While it was functioning correctly the 17 made a splendid road car, an occasional inclination of the wrists being entirely adequate for the majority of corners and overtaking manoeuvres. Both performance and noise level were exhilarating, to say the least, and the ride was very good in view of the car's basic purpose. Lack of vertical space made its strut-type front suspension rather less satisfactory on circuits.

The first rear-engined sports/racer was the 23, and my reactions to it after a drive round Goodwood were much the same as to the 18 and 20—it didn't fit me. But even so, and even though it had only an 1100cc pushrod Ford engine, it was obviously a far better circuit car than the 17 and I was not at all surprised when the late Jimmy Clark, driving a 1000cc twin cam 23, put all the bigger cars to shame in the early stages of the 1962 Nurburgring 1000km.

It was several months after the announcement before I managed to get my hands on a Lotus Elan, and when I did finally collect one I only got as far as Waltham Abbey before it boiled. A telephone call to the factory service department elicited the information that they had no transport and couldn't I drive it back?—which I finally managed after topping up with water twice in three miles. A few days later the Elan returned, this time with the water hose connected to the radiator, and ran faultlessly for a week. However, I was a little disappointed with it, and in particular with the noise level and fuel consumption (yes, I ran out of petrol again).

In 1966 I borrowed a series two Elan for the trip to the Turin show, and it really was a completely different motor car. Driven really hard the Elan chassis has some limitations, but for fast touring—and I mean fast—it is a wonderfully safe and enjoyable car to drive.

The Elan +2 seems to be very much the In car at the present moment, and an amazing number—many of them with special paint finishes—are to be seen in the more fashionable parts of London. I must arrange to borrow one for a long trip as soon as Colin Chapman can scrape up enough cash for a full tank of petrol . . .

NEW AT GENEVA

NEW LOTUS SEVEN SERIES 4

JUST when spring seems only around the corner, Lotus have introduced a revised Seven two-seater, a car for fine weather if ever there was one. Our test of the Lotus Seven Twin-Cam appeared on 29 January this year; a lot of the points we criticized have now been improved.

The new car uses a fully stressed steel frame—without the aluminium skin panels of the earlier version—with a new moulded glass-fibre body and some suspension revisions. It looks much more modern with a kind of "street buggy" appearance.

Fabricated steel sheet is used for the front section of the chassis, with a tubular frame around the central cockpit area and at the rear. Instead of locating the live rear axle on trailing arms and an A-bracket, the new version uses a Watt linkage each side, with the right-hand trailing link triangulated to form a wide-based single wishbone.

Front suspension is now just like that of the Europa, with pressed steel members instead of forged ones. Rack and pinion steering is much the same as before except that a collapsible Triumph Herald column is used.

The new body is formed by a one-piece moulding which forms the main floor pan, the double skinned cockpit sides, the tail section and the main scuttle. Front wings are sweeping and separate mouldings which flow right back to meet the rear wheelarch bulges. The whole bonnet top and nose section now hinges forward, greatly improving engine accessibility.

As before there is choice of Ford engines, ranging from a standard 1600 GT 84 bhp unit to a Holbay-tuned twin-cam giving 135 bhp.

No price has been announced as we close for press, but this is expected to be decided in time for the Geneva Show presentation.

Still with same kind of characteristic appearance, the new Lotus Seven is much more habitable and sleeker in profile. Frame construction and suspension have been modified

Ton-up lightweight

Reborn 7 with stylish glassfibre body and better cockpit; tractable Cortina GT engine; exhilarating to drive; precise agile handling, skittish in wet; excellent gearbox but heavy clutch; quite expensive as a stark kit car

It used to be easy to spot the owner of a Lotus 7; he was agile, perhaps even a contortionist, walked with a stoop, had a damp right sleeve and a watery eye. He was a die-hard wind-in-the-face enthusiast prepared to sacrifice all, or nearly all, creature comforts and convenience in pursuit of performance and the pleasure of driving an open sports car in its simplest and perhaps purest form.

Lotus mark numbers are now up to 72, so the 7 was clearly an early one. In fact it is 13 years since it first saw the light of day. Since then it has remained the epitome of a fun car and until this year had changed very little apart from the fitting of a succession of different engines into the light, simple tubular space-frame in accordance with the latest thinking at Dagenham.

It is an open secret that Lotus have been trying to kill the 7 for some time. It was not really an economic proposition under the new set-up at Hethel and hardly in keeping with the image of performance with refinement set by the Elan and Europa. That it survives today is largely due to the efforts of Graham Nearn of Caterham Car Sales who obtained the sole concession for the 7 some years ago. It was he who put up the idea of civilizing and glamorizing the little tin box for its series 4 form. He plans to sell 250 kits this year.

Inevitably some people will say that the car has gone soft and lost much of its character in the revisions which include a stylish one-piece glassfibre body in place of the previous conglomorate of mouldings and alloy panels; a completely new console and facia with instruments designed to be read on the move; and more comprehensive easy-to-work protection against the elements. There is now hardly a bare frame tube in sight since the whole of the interior is lined with a neat black moulding to give a monocoque effect. The seats are still not adjustable, and you either fit or you don't, but they are now comfortably shaped and no longer cushions laid on the floor.

We didn't think it had lost any of its appeal as a fun car; in fact the more aggressive shape of the new body would, we think, do far more to win friends and influence people than the old one. It is slightly heavier than the last we tested and the standard crossflow 1600 unit develops a little less power than the tweaked 1500 Classic engine used then. But it will still reach a genuine maximum of 100 mph, scorch up to 60 mph in under 9s and pull strongly from as low as 15 mph in top gear. This should be

Price: £950 (component form only, no purchase tax); magnesium alloy wheels £42; heater £17; roll-over bar £15; screen washers £3 5s; air horns £4 15s; tonneau cover £10; Price as tested £1042
Make: Lotus. Model 7 SE. Makers: Lotus Components Ltd, Norwich, NOR 92W.

good enough for most fun seekers; if not the latest engine options include the Holbay Clubman and the Special Equipment twin-cam.

The ride is surprisingly good for this kind of car though there is still a trace of scuttle shake. Too much power through a bumpy corner will lurch it off line and it tends to slide around like a bar of soap in the bath on wet roads. Otherwise, it goes where it's pointed and its inherent swervability and light, direct steering are ideal for jinking in and out of traffic. Although the car is a lot more civilised than before most of our criticism still relates to the total lack of amenities. There is space for no more luggage than the proverbial week-end suitcase, rather less with the hood down; and once the neat rear tonneau is in place there is nowhere to stow even a packet of Polo. With the hood up clambering in and out through the small opening afforded by the hinged side screens is tiresome. The screens themselves are fiddly to release from inside and we lost count of the number of techniques adopted by young ladies attempting to enter the car with a degree of decorum; none were successful. The new hood no longer has three-quarter panels so visibility has suffered. But perhaps this doesn't matter to the damp-sleeve fraternity.

The 7 was built to give pleasure from the moment the lorry dumps the formidable pile of seemingly unrelated parts in your front garden. Considering that all of the £950 it costs goes to Lotus and none to the government, it may seem rather expensive fun but even after 13 years there are still no serious imitations.

Performance and economy

First impressions can be misleading. With its rakish lines, prominent outside exhaust curling away from the fabricated bunch-of-bananas system, and obvious performance potential we expected the 7 to be fierce and raucous, our bright red test car to be an immediate target for every copper in Z division. It is fierce certainly, as we would expect with a power/weight ratio of 150 bhp per ton, but after the harsh bellow of the Cosworth 1500 with its twin 40 DCOE Webers, the standard 1600 cross-flow unit is almost an anticlimax. Some enthusiasts might even say it was too quiet; we thought the level about right and it was a pleasant change to drive a sports car which was as tractable and

PERFORMANCE

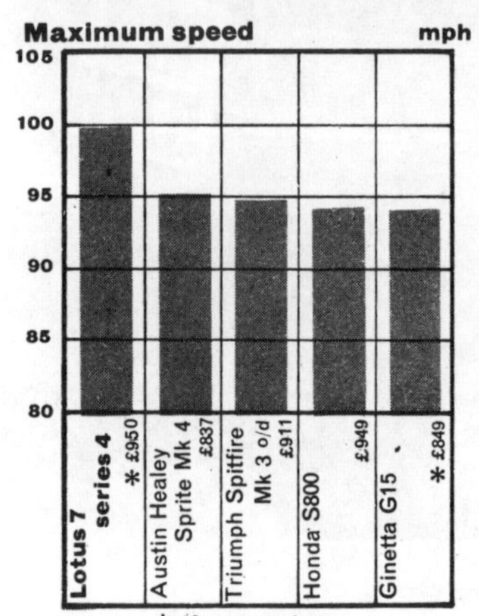

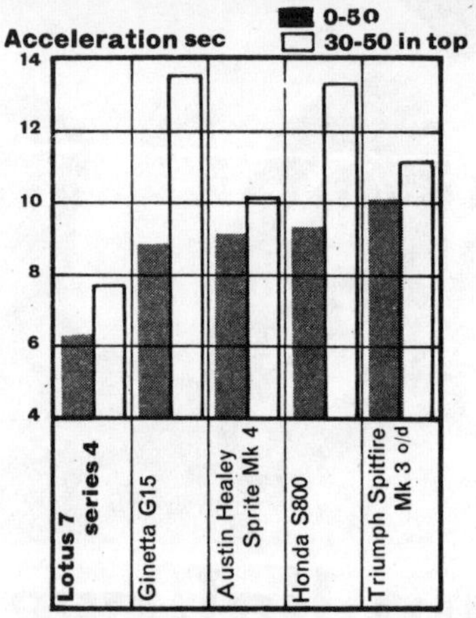

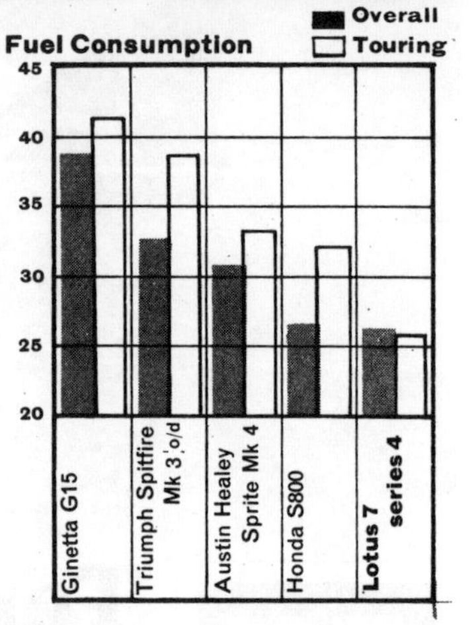

* Component form

Performance tests carried out by *Motor's* staff at the Motor Industry Research Association proving ground, Lindley.

Conditions

Weather: Warm and dry, wind 10-12 mph
Temperature: 56-60°F
Barometer: 29.6 in. hg.
Surface: Dry tarmacadam
Fuel: 98 octane (RM) 4-Star rating

Maximum Speeds

		mph	kph
Mean lap banked circuit		100	161
Best one-way ¼-mile		108.5	175
Direct top gear	at 6500 rpm		
3rd gear		82	132
2nd gear		58	93
1st gear		39	63

"Maximile" speed: (Timed quarter mile after 1 mile accelerating from rest)

Mean	99.1
Best	101.2

Acceleration Times

mph	sec
0-30	3.0
0-40	4.5
0-50	6.3
0-60	8.8
0-70	11.8
0-80	16.0
0-90	24.2
Standing quarter mile	16.0
Standing Kilometer	31.4

mph	Top sec.	3rd sec.
10-30	—	5.2
20-40	7.1	4.8
30-50	7.2	4.5
40-60	7.5	4.5
50-70	7.9	5.3
60-80	9.3	7.6
70-90	13.0	—

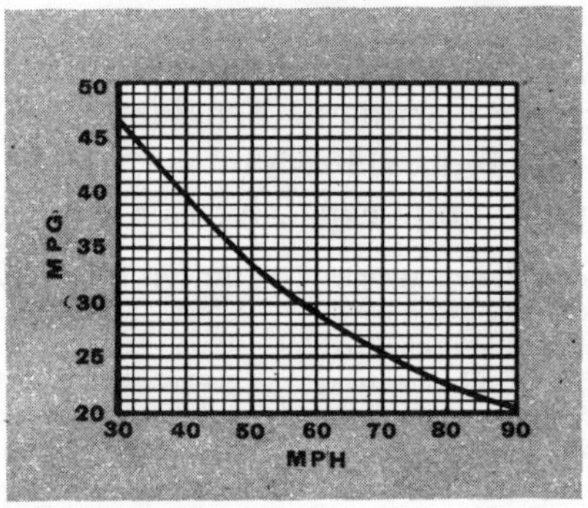

Fuel Consumption

Touring (consumption midway between 30 mph and maximum less 5 per cent allowance for acceleration) 25.9 mpg
Overall 26.3 mpg
(=10.8 litres/100km)
Total test distance 1460 miles

Brakes

Pedal pressure, deceleration and equivalent stopping distance from 30 mph

lb.	g.	ft.
25	0.38	79
50	1+	30
Handbrake	0.30	100

Fade Test

20 stops at ½g deceleration at 1 min. intervals from a speed midway between 40 mph and maximum speed (=70 mph)

	lb.
Pedal force at beginning	30
Pedal force at 10th stop	30
Pedal force at 20th stop	30

Steering

Turning circle between kerbs:

	ft.
Left	30½
Right	29½

Turns of steering wheel from lock to lock 2¾
Steering wheel deflection for 50 ft. diameter circle 0.8 turns

Clutch

Free pedal movement ½in.
Additional movement to disengage clutch completely 2in.
Maximum pedal load 50lb.

Speedometer

Indicated	30	40	50	60	70	80	90
True	29	39	49	58	67½	76	85

Distance recorder 2 per cent fast

Weight

Kerb weight (unladen with fuel for approximately 50 miles) 11.4 cwt
Front/rear distribution 48½/51½
Weight laden as tested 15.2cwt

Parkability

Gap needed to clear 6 ft. wide obstruction in front 4ft. 11 in.

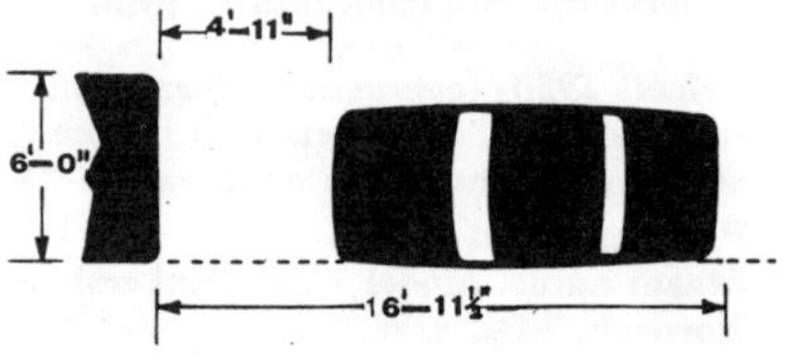

unobtrusive in city traffic as it was exhilarating when given its head on the open road.

The GT engine with the normal compound Weber downdraught carburetter produces 84 bhp at 5400 rpm compared with 95 bhp at 6000 rpm of the old Cosworth 1500. Torque is about the same, 92 lb.ft., but it reaches a maximum much lower down, at only 3600 rpm which makes it a much more docile and tractable unit. The cross-flow engine is not noted for smoothness; in fact with the light weight and firm engine mounts of the 7 it tends to be rather harsh throughout its range, though there are no serious vibration periods or flat spots and it will pull cleanly and strongly in top gear from speeds at which many sports car engines would be trying to jump out of the bonnet: witness the 30-50 mph top gear time of 7.7 seconds. Breathing seems rather restricted at the top end and the engine seemed reluctant to rev in the orange sector of the rev counter which ends at 6500 rpm. This has little effect on acceleration, though, especially as hard standing starts are easy.

Our best mean lap of MIRA in rather blustery conditions was exactly 100 mph but we managed a best quarter of over 108 mph with an engine that was still a little on the tight side. The car did not like being held at high speeds for long though; either the air intake is inadequate or it chokes itself at speed since even after a fairly short spell at 85-90 mph the temperature climbs well above normal and the oil pressure settled to 25 psi or less, enough to make the more mechanically sympathetic lift off. Fortunately readings returned to normal very quickly.

We were a little surprised that the 7 did not return a better touring consumption figure than 25.9 mpg for cruising at 65 mph although an overall figure of 26.3 mpg is pretty good for a sports car driven hard. Even so the range with the eight gallon tank is only a little over 200 miles. Refuelling is not the nuisance it used to be now that the filler cap has been moved from the floor of the luggage compartment to an external position in the nearside wing. Being a standard engine, it is virtually free of temperament and runs quite happily on four-star petrol.

Transmission

The excellent 2000E semi-close ratio gearbox is a standard fitting on the SE model we tested. There is no frictional resistance or

Thanks to easy entry into an open cockpit, above, our man made a clean getaway on this occasion. Inside, below, it's a snug fit

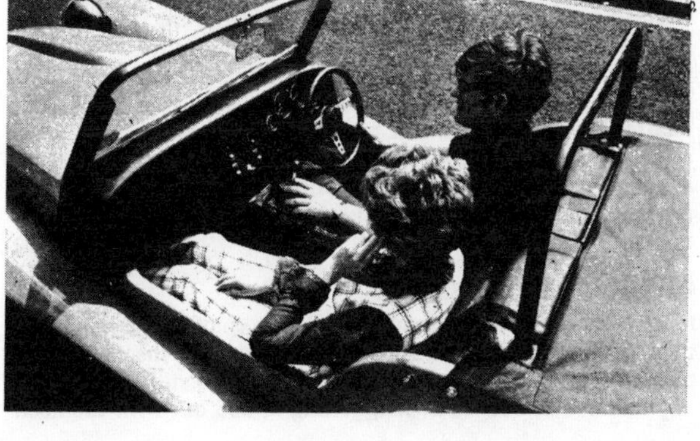

The fixed seats are comfortably bolstered and provide a good driving position if you're not tall. The handbrake fouls your knee

Still starkly functional, above, but striking and not inelegant

Hood and sidescreens can be stowed in the "boot", above, leaving little room for other luggage. Erecting the hood, below, is a fairly quick but fiddly process with all those pop fasteners

free-play in the sturdy gearlever and the synchromesh is unbeatable yet hardly notchy, let alone obstructive. Our only complaint is that the very narrow gate sometimes leads to snicking reverse on the way down into second. We liked the ratios of this box, too, particularly the uprated second gear which can hurl the car up to nearly 60 mph. After flirtations with various final drives (Graham Nearn once used to scour the dealers for spare Standard 10 axles) Lotus have now settled on the 3.77 to 1 Escort axle which gives 17.8 mph per 1000 rpm in top gear, a reasonably long-legged cruising ratio.

Compared with the change the clutch is intolerably heavy; it needs a push of 50 lb. to release completely. Fortunately only the slightest dip of the pedal is required to effect a smooth change, but it is a good cure for drivers who ride the clutch at traffic lights. The car started easily on the 1 in 3 test hill.

Handling and brakes

Since the 7 was first made, Colin Chapman has gone on to show in cars like the Elan that superlative handling can be combined with an acceptably soft ride. The 7 remains comparatively wooden, though it doesn't jar even on very bad surfaces. But it is firm enough for the road surface to have a fairly significant influence on cornering behaviour.

The front suspension now consists mainly of Europa components but that at the rear is completely new and best described as a double Watts linkage, with trailing links to the bottom of the axle and leading links from a rearward extension to the chassis. It relies heavily on rubber bushes for compliance, an A-bracket for lateral location, and the geometry is such that roll is resisted by twist on the axle case which thus serves as a giant anti-roll bar.

On smooth surfaces, the handling is very neutral, the fat Dunlop SP sport tyres have tremendous adhesion and the car can simply be steered round on a steady throttle at seemingly impossible speeds. Put the power on too early and the car is undecided whether to plough straight on with understeer or push the tail out. The result, a rather untidy lurching motion and a lot of tyre squeal. If the road is bumpy, the back end always goes first as the tyres patter and lose adhesion and very high rear roll stiffness unloads the inside wheel. Roll is very well controlled, virtually non-existent, but there still seems to be some lateral movement in the rear suspension as there was evidence of the near side rear tyre having fouled the wheel arch after our performance tests.

Though our only chance to try the 7 in the wet came after a prolonged dry spell when the roads can be treacherously slippery, we were not impressed with wet road adhesion; considerable care was needed with the throttle to keep the rear end in check. The steering is very light and direct—$2\frac{3}{4}$ turns lock to lock and 0.8 turns for the 50ft. circle—but it lacks self-centring which makes it feel rather dead at times. Rough surfaces cause some dither and kick-back which it is sometimes necessary to minimize by holding the wheel between finger and thumb on the spokes. Although the new body is now much stronger, and the wings and headlights no longer vibrate, there is still enough whip in the chassis to produce scuttle shake. Undoubtedly the 7 is at its best on fairly smooth twisty roads on which it is as manoeuvrable and exhilarating to drive as perhaps any car in the world. Being so light it builds up very little momentum through a series of bends and it can be swerved under complete control almost as fast as the driver can turn the wheel. The same attributes coupled with the exceptional tractability of the engine also make it extremely easy to get around town in heavy traffic.

The brakes are not servoed but still extremely effective, 50 lb. pedal pressure being sufficient to produce a 1g stop. They were unaffected by our fade test and recovered almost immediately after a soaking in the water splash. Admittedly in need of adjustment the pistol-grip handbrake is still an unsolved problem; we doubt that it could ever be made to hold the car on the 1 in 3 slope.

Comfort and controls

Lotus 7 customers presumably don't list comfort very high on their priorities. It is designed purely as an instrument of pleasure, an objective it achieves superbly. It is still cramped for any driver over 5ft. 10in. tall; getting in and out with the hood

SPECIFICATION

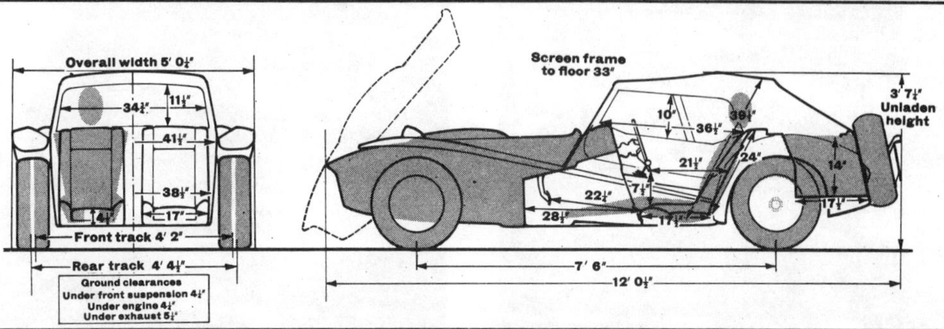

1600 cc front engine driving rear wheels through live axle; tubular and sheet steel frame; separate glassfibre body

Engine

Block material	Cast iron
Head material	Cast iron
Cylinders	4
Cooling system	Water
Bore and stroke	8.98 mm (3.188in.) 77.62 mm (3.056in.)
Cubic capacity	1599 cc (97.6 cu. in.)
Main bearings	5
Valves	Pushrod ohv
Compression ratio	9:1
Carburetter	Weber compound downdraught
Fuel pump	AC mechanical
Oil filter	Full flow
Max. power (net)	84 bhp at 5500 rpm
Max. torque (net)	96 lb. ft. at 3600 rpm

Transmission

Clutch	8-in. sdp diaphragm
Internal gear box ratios	
Top gear	1.00
3rd gear	1.40
2nd gear	2.01
1st gear	2.97
Reverse	3.32
Synchromesh	All forward gears
Final drive	3.77:1
Mph at 1000 rpm in:	
Top gear	17.8
3rd gear	12.7
2nd gear	8.9
1st gear	6.0

Chassis and body

Construction	Tubular chassis with stressed steel side panels, sheet steel front assembly, glassfibre body bolted on with separate front wings and bonnet

Brakes

Type	Disc/drum
Dimensions	9in. diameter discs front 9in. diameter drums rear
Friction areas:	
Front	14.7 sq. in. of lining operating on 34.6 sq. in. of disc
Rear	47.2 sq. in. of lining operating on 99 sq. in. of drum

Suspension and steering

Front	Double wishbones and coil springs
Rear	Live axle located by double Watts linkage and coil springs
Shock absorbers	Telescopic front and rear
Steering type	Rack and pinion
Tyres	165 x 13 HR Dunlop Sport Radial
Wheels	Pressed steel disc (alloy wheels optional)
Rim size	5½J

Coachwork and equipment

Starting handle	No
Tool kit contents	Spare wheel kit (optional extra)
Jack	Screw scissors
Jacking points	Under chassis side rails
Battery	12 volt negative earth 35 amp hrs capacity
Number of electrical fuses	2
Headlamps	60/45 watt sealed beam
Indicators	Self cancelling flashers
Reversing lamp	No
Screen wipers	Two speed electric
Screen washers	Electric (optional extra)
Sun visors	No
Locks:	
With ignition key	Ignition only
Interior heater	Recirculating (optional)
Upholstery	Ambla
Floor covering	Rubber mats
Alternative body styles	None
Maximum load	1650 lbs all up weight
Maximum roof rack load	None

Maintenance

Fuel tank capacity	7½ galls
Sump	5.8 pints SAE 10/30
Gearbox	2.4 pints SAE 80 EP
Rear axle	2 pints SAE 90 EP
Steering gear	0.25 pint SAE 90 hypoid
Coolant	12 pints (1 drain plug)
Chassis lubrication	None
Minimum service interval	6000 miles
Ignition timing	
Contact breaker gap	0.025in.
Sparking plug gap	0.023in.
Sparking plug type	Autolite AG22A 14 mm
Tappet clearance (hot)	Inlet 0.0012in. Exhaust 0.022in.
Valve timing:	
inlet opens	27° btdc
inlet closes	65° abdc
exhaust opens	65° bbdc
exhaust closes	27° atdc
Front wheel toe-in	0–1/16in.
Camber angle	0°
Castor angle	5°
King pin inclination	8½°
Tyre pressures:	
Front	16 psi
Rear	22 psi

Safety check list

Steering Assembly	
Steering box position	in front of engine
Steering column collapsible	yes
Steering wheel boss padded	no
Steering wheel dished	yes
Instrument Panel	
Projecting switches	no
Sharp cowls	no
Padding	none
Windscreen and Visibility	
Screen type	laminated
Pillars padded	no
Standard driving mirrors	interior
Interior mirror framed	yes
Interior mirror collapsible	no
Sun visors	none
Seats and Harness	
Attachment to floor	permanently fixed
Do they tip forward?	no
Head rest attachment points	no
Safety harness	lap and diagonal

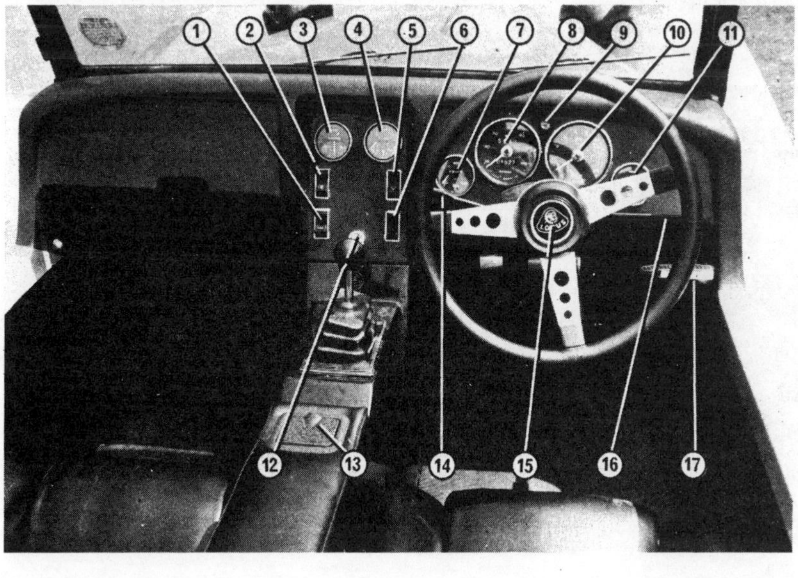

1 heater boost fan. 2 side lights. 3 ammeter. 4 fuel gauge. 5 wipers. 6 electric washers (optional). 7 temperature gauge. 8 speedometer with trip and total mileage recorders. 9 indicator tell-tale. 10 rev counter. 11 oil pressure gauge. 12 ignition/starter switch. 13 ash tray. 14 main/dip/flasher stalk. 15 horn. 16 indicator stalk. 17 handbrake.

Rear threequarter visibility is hampered by absence of side panels

The sidescreens hinge forward but the roof is low and the sill high

up calls for considerable agility; and the toe-board is so narrow that it is unwise to attempt to drive fast without proper driving shoes. Otherwise the car has been refined about as thoroughly and effectively as it could be without sacrificing any of its sporting character. In addition to the one-piece glassfibre body the redesigned chassis now has sheet steel sections along the cockpit sides and farther forward to provide mounts for the front suspension. The cockpit seems to be completely waterproof. It is also slightly bigger with more elbow room and an extra 2½in. in the wheelbase, most of which has gone into the cockpit. As a result most people will now be able to hold the neat and comfortable leather rimmed steering wheel at arms' length without hanging their right elbow over the side.

The new seats are still fixed but extremely comfortable and support the occupants rather than simply wedge them in place. With the left arm resting comfortably on the padded transmission tunnel the gearlever is perfectly placed though most people will want more leg room or somewhere to rest the left foot off the clutch without having to bend the knee. Otherwise the pedals are well placed for heel-and-toe changes.

The car is most pleasant to drive with the hood off and the sidescreens in place; there is too much draught round the sides of the windscreen when these are removed. In this form entry is quite easy; a single fastener allows the screen to pivot like a front-hinged door and you climb in over the side without too much difficulty. The new wings now extend right down to meet the rear wheel arches so there is no longer any risk of passengers burning their legs on the outside exhaust which used to be rather exposed on that side. The new screens have sliding Perspex windows but it is still a rather fiddly job to reach the fastener from inside the car.

The hood is well made and fits snugly, making a watertight seal with the screens. But with more than a dozen poppet fasteners to do up it is necessary to anticipate a shower well in advance.

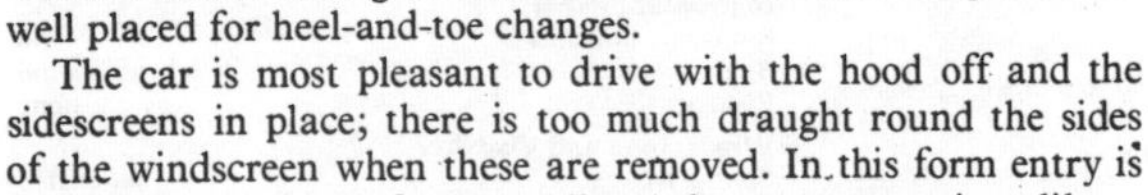

1 dipstick. 2 electric air horns (optional). 3 voltage regulator. 4 clutch reservoir. 5 brake fluid reservoir. 6 fuel pump. 7 carburetter. 8 distributor. 9 coil.

With the hood up the car is now quite cosy; provided the screens are tensioned to press firmly against the body sides very few draughts intrude and nobody complained of getting wet. Visibility to the sides and rear is good—until the Perspex gets scratched, which it will in time. The elimination of the clear panels from the rear corners seriously cuts visibility in that direction and you have to cut across road junctions at right angles, Europa fashion, to be able to see what's coming. Getting out of a closed 7 is laborious and inelegant especially as the angle of the screen hinges stops them staying open.

Luggage room is restricted to the well behind the seats into which the hood and its folding frame must be fitted when the car is open. With careful planning it should be possible to stow a fair sized suitcase and some soft baggage on top of the hood and then secure it neatly with the tonneau which is permanently attached behind the seats. With this in place there is nowhere to put a map or the odd bar of chocolate out of sight—annoying as there is room behind the new facia panel to incorporate a locker or cubby on the passenger's side.

Fittings and furniture

The new facia is neat and attractive with speedometer, rev counter, oil pressure and water temperature gauges immediately in front of the driver. A centre console contains the ammeter and a fuel gauge (a new addition to the equipment) and piano key switches for the wipers, electric washers, side lights and heater. As usual with the Herald steering column there are two stalks, for indicators on the right and main beam dip and flash on the left. Climate control is strictly limited; there is no means of ventilation and the heater is a simple recirculating unit with a tap under the bonnet, a single speed fan, and no provision to demist the windscreen. Still, it does seem possible to provide enough heat to warm the tiny cockpit very quickly when necessary. Among the external modifications are separate direction indicators beside the radiator intake with repeaters on the wings, moulded-in parking lights and much more elegant rear light clusters incorporated in the rakish squared-off tail. Safety has not been neglected either; lap and diagonal seat belts are very well mounted and comfortable to wear and a substantial rollover bar is an optional extra and a reminder of the 7's racing ancestry. The headlights have very good range and spread.

Accessibility and maintenance

The whole of the front section of the new body now hinges forward on releasing a catch at the base of the windscreen. It checks open with a strut and fully exposes the engine and front suspension. No chassis maintenance is required except for occasional oiling of clevis pins and cables, but the engine requires the usual Ford service schedule and oil change every 6000 miles. No tools are included as standard but a roll containing jack and wheel changing equipment is offered as an optional extra for £3 10s.

LOTUS SEVEN S4

The no-nonsense concept is the same, but mechanically it's a brand-new car

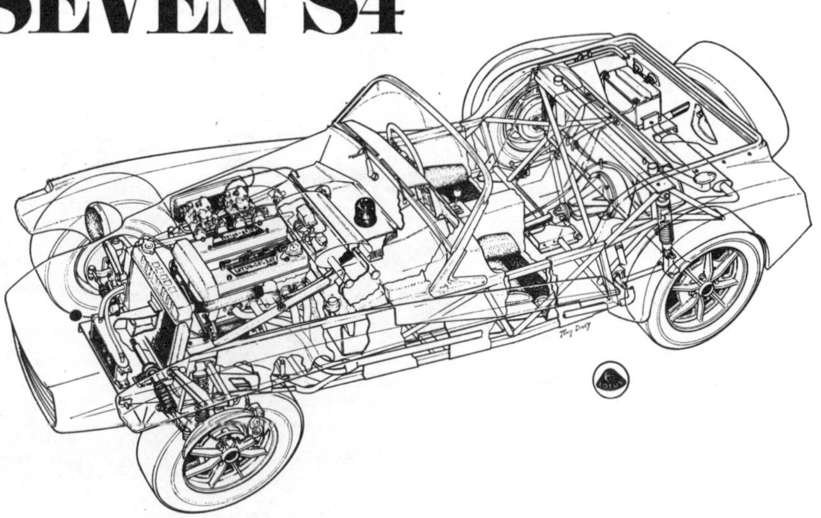

BY CYRIL POSTHUMUS

STRANGE HOW LOTUS, epitome of ultra-clean, efficient car design when it comes to racing single-seaters, can produce something as homely looking as the Seven. But they do, and despite announcing about two years ago that production of this first Lotus production model was to end, they changed their mind a few weeks later and kept it coming off the line. But now at last, in its 13th year, they have brought it up to date—maybe not in appearance, but it's much more modern under the skin.

It now has a completely stressed tubular steel chassis to which is bolted a fiberglass body; and that body gives more legroom, has a one-piece forward-hinged hood and front suspension by double wishbones and coil springs *à la* Europa. Rear axle is still a live affair, located by rubber-bushed lower trailing A-arms and upper trailing arms, the lot controlled by coil spring/damper units all round. Burman rack-and-pinion steering is fitted, and safety features include collapsible steering column, an optional roll-over bar, flush rocker switches, hazard light, specially mounted windshield and Dunlop Aquajet tires. The dashboard has been ergonomically designed and has anti-glare trim, while generous soundproofing and new folding top make the car less stark.

It is called the Seven S (for Series) 4 and the engine is a Ford 1600 GT which gives 84 bhp at 5800 rpm, with the option of the 1300 Escort GT unit or the Lotus-Holbay twincam 1558-cc engine. The latter gives the little car 0-50 mph acceleration in 4.9 sec and 0-70 mph in just over 9 sec. The Holbay engine can be had with mods giving up to 135 bhp, which in a car weighing a little over 1000 lb promises *real* performance. Factory-fitted optional extras include limited-slip diff, close-ratio gearbox, luxury trim, full harness seat belts, Brand Lotus alloy wheels with Goodyear 195 x 13 rally tires, etc. A real clubman's competition car, this one. Dimensions are: length, 146 in., height 44 in., width 61 in. The 9-gallon tank is behind the seats, protected by the chassis.

The car will be available both in kit form and as a complete car, and plans are now being completed to market it in the U.S. Price of the new car has not been settled yet. Main external differences from the old Seven lie in the tail treatment and the front mudguards, though these still extend rearward in old MG style. The radiator intake is somewhat austere and rectangular, and would (I think, anyway) look nicer with a wedge shape.

Standard engine is Cortina GT of 84 bhp DIN—cutaway above shows Holbay twincam.

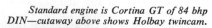

RUMBLINGS

"Having been flown up on the Sunday (to Hethel), we thought it only decent to depart in a Lotus." The Editor about to drive from Norfolk to Radnorshire in the latest Lotus 7.

■ **LIVING WITH THE LOTUS 7.**—In May, to attract people to Wymondham to see the Group Lotus Car Companies' factories and to raise funds for the Norwich Lads' Club, Graham Hill opened the Lotus Open Weekend of 1970, at which a display of historic Lotus cars, modern Lotus cars, a fairground, midget car racing, a flying display which included a visit by a Hurricane, a dance, and other jollies were laid on. Having been flown up on the Sunday in a Piper Twin Commanche, appropriately one wearing a competition number, a legacy from the London-Sydney race, we thought it only decent to depart in a Lotus. Which we did, in a Series 4 Seven, scorning to erect the hood, so that the journey to Wales tied in with what we wrote last month about sports cars and the joys of open-air motoring . . .

It was our intention to write about what it is like to live with a Lotus 7 but there wasn't one to spare, the car we borrowed being the personal property of Mike Warner, Managing Director of Lotus Components Ltd., which had to be returned within the week. However, it is possible from this necessarily brief encounter to convey something of what this cheeky little modern sports car is like.

We realised almost as soon as the security police had permitted us to get out on to the road that the Lotus 7 puts the fun back into motoring in no uncertain manner. But the smooth, quiet running of the car and its civilised suspension came as a surprise. The accelerator is in close proximity to the foot-brake and maybe because Warner's car was very new (it showed only 527 miles on its odometer) the gear-change was extraordinarily stiff, third impossibly baulky, and the clutch very "sudden". That apart, the Lotus 7 is simplicity to drive, the short central gear lever well placed, the steering very light and responsive to scarcely more than wrist movements, 2⅝ turns of the little leather-rimmed wheel taking it from one full lock to the other. This example had the Cortina GT engine, which ran quietly, with a subdued exhaust note, yet when the throttle was opened things happened—fast, the little red two-seater accelerating to the eager note of efficient machinery. The car's light weight (10 cwt. 3 qr. empty, but with about four gallons of fuel) is reflected in the ready response to the accelerator even in top gear. At 70 m.p.h. the tachometer reads just below 4,000 r.p.m. and an indicated 100 m.p.h. comes up quite quickly.

There is nothing dramatic about driving this Seven, apart from steering shake as the wheel plays through one's fingers and some frenzy from the bonnet and the "power-bulge" in front of the driver, which can reflect the sun into one's eyes. It is not to be compared to vintage motoring and, indeed, offers fewer amenities. It is, however, enormous fun, and light though it is to handle, it provides plenty of exercise, because, being doorless, getting in and out becomes a bit athletic—and may well have been planned with mini-skirts in mind! The detachable sidescreens serve as doors but to release them an awkwardly-placed single external turn-stud has to be manipulated through the sliding window and there is nothing to hold up the "door" as you climb out. Getting out when the hood is up must be almost impossible, and quite claustrophobic . . .

The seats, like those on early Morgan Plus Fours, are fixed (but the pedals can be adjusted). On the Lotus they are a snug but not very comfortable fit, because you lie rather than sit in them, but not to the extent that a racing driver lies in a GP car, so driving the Seven can put a bit of a strain on the lumbar muscles. But snug fit they are, to the extent of leaving the seat harness to be sat on unless it is worn (the Lotus belts were easy to use, says W.B.'s wife) and with the side pieces up there is not much elbow room. Provision for a tonneau cover would have been appreciated.

Otherwise, this Seven is very civilised. Hood and sidescreens stow in the boot, which has a cover easy to fit thanks to Tenax fasteners, which are an improvement of "lift-the-dots" as well as being neater, although one pulled out of the fabric. There is full, easy to read, Smith's instrumentation (heat 70 to 80°C.), a Smith's Series 3 heater, and winkers with side repeaters on the front mudguards—and they are *real* mudguards. Four press-buttons on the centre panel work lights, heater-fan, wipers and washers. The bonnet releases absurdly easily to hinge forward and reveal most of the mechanism, including the Weber carburetter topped by a Nordic air-cleaner. The finish of the fibreglass body is excellent and the frog's-eyes Lucas headlamps, black on this car in contrast to the red paintwork, give an effective beam. The spare wheel lives on the tail (Dunlop SP Sport radials were fitted), there is a quick-action fuel filler in the broad n/s rear wing, and the Lotus 7 comes with roll-over bar, ready to race.

Leaving Norfolk on our solo drive to Wales we were soon making good progress along the A11, picking off the dodderers with impressive bursts of effortless acceleration. It was very much open-air motoring, however, in the bitter gale that was sweeping off Thetford heath and Newmarket plain and in the Snetterton area (where a race meeting was presumably in progress for a Chain-Gang Frazer Nash was seen abandoned on the adjacent straight). We endured the buffeting from the wind until St. Neots, before pausing to erect the side bits, which plug in easily and make open-car motoring much less tough. (Sports cars of the 1920s didn't habitually go at the pace we were extracting from the Lotus and their aero screens probably created less back-draught than the Lotus' upright one.) In the softer country beyond Bedford the run became extremely pleasant, for there is nothing quite like this Seven, which rattles and shakes a bit but clings to the road like a limpet and steers with the accuracy of a micrometer. The 258-mile journey was accomplished well within the six-hour target in spite of several more pauses, to map-read and refuel, and much crawling Sunday traffic with which to contend. The fuel gauge went to zero just before Tewkesbury, suggesting a usable range of some 200 miles, at very roughly 30 m.p.g. The gear-change got progressively more horrid, however, until it was almost impossible to shift, due to clutch drag, which adjusting the pedal wouldn't cure (to do which a country garage charged at the rate of 45s. an hour!), but the adequate ground clearance up the rough house-drive that marked journey's end was another pleasant surprise, although eventually the exhaust tail-pipe bracket fractured.

This short acquaintance with Mr. Chapman's boy's-racer confirmed what enormous fun the latest Seven is (until the transmission went solid) and now we want to try the hotter twin-cam version.

44-17-1

Ideal for the 23-year-old bachelor, and a boost to those not so fortunate in years, the 7 remains much the same since its announcement in 1957.

Learning to love the 7

Most Lotus cars are mechanically up to the minute. But there is one model in the range which, despite some fairly extensive modifications last year, remains essentially the same as when it was announced in 1957. Even then the designer of the Lotus 7 must have forgotten to change his calendar for many years. Along with Peter Morgan's well-loved cars, the Seven is the last of a dying breed of windswept, bumpy, fast, exhilarating, awkward, lovable sports cars.

It is an impractical car which an owner would come to accept, love and cherish. I have a friend who has owned one for several years. Although he is not a typical Seven owner — that's a 23-year-old single man according to David Wakefield, a director of Caterham Cars — his attitude is characteristic. His car is old enough to have been the first off the assembly line. It has an old 1-litre BMC engine, has been involved in at least one major accident, regularly shakes many of the nuts loose, has farcical weather protection and is the veritable apple of its owner's eye.

He tells fisherman-like fibs about its performance and reliability, spends hours fiddling, adjusting, modifying, drives the breadth of Britain in all weathers with the hood down, fishing rods tucked heaven knows where. I used to regard his attitude as eccentric. Frankly, after a spell with the latest Series 4 I have more understanding and sympathy.

While driving the car I adopted John Bolster's maxim of imagining myself as the typical owner. The Seven did not suit my family needs but it would ideally suit those of that 23-year-old bachelor. First, it is a Lotus, born and bred by a tremendously successful racing car constructor. Cars that have this sort of heritage tend to have good seating positions, steering, road-holding, performance. The Seven certainly has those, and if there isn't a plastic wood-style fascia, what matter!

The current Seven, whose ancestry goes back to the Lotus Mk 6, has a pigmented glassfibre body around the familiar strong tubular/sheet steel chassis. It has a more square look than the older alloy-bodied versions. Access to the engine is complete as the whole bonnet lifts forward.

Front suspension is by twin pressed steel wishbones with coil spring/damper units and an anti-roll bar. At the rear is a live axle located by trailing and leading links and equipped with coil spring/damper units. Front brakes are 8½ in discs and at the rear there are 9 in drums. The attractive 5½J alloy wheels are fitted with 165 x 13 Dunlop Sport radial tyres.

The canvas and perspex doors open completely, and there is a definite knack to getting in. (It's a real test of girl's elegance.) The low slung PVC seats are extremely comfortable, and with the padding, transmission tunnel and body sides, there is no question of being thrown about in cornering. You get in and are simply wedged there, in the nicest possible way.

The fascia is matt black plastic. Why put in anything more fancy if it's only going to be rained on? The Smiths instruments reveal all one needs to know—speed of the engine, speed of the car, oil pressure, water temperature, how much petrol is left in the rear-mounted 7½ gallon tank and the state of the battery. There are rocker switches to control the two-speed windscreen wipers, the washers, heater (what are Sevens coming to!) and side and main lights. Further lighting control is on the steering column, along with the direction indicators.

The 13 in PVC-bound steering wheel contains a Lotus badge on the boss, just to remind you of the type of car you are driving. With that fabulous Burman rack and pinion steering, who could forget? Lap and diagonal seat belts are fitted, and there are mounting points for full shoulder harness. Just behind the driver's head a stout roll-over bar sprouts out of the chassis. A sheet of canvas at the back neatly covers the hood when not in use—which it rarely is—and the small luggage space.

The seating position suited me perfectly. The steering wheel was the right distance

The cockpit is a snug fit and data that one needs to know is well presented by ample instrumentation.
44-17-2

"The rear wheels began to bite immediately the critical point was reached." 44-17-3

away and the short, notchy gear lever a few inches away. The good handbrake is of the umbrella variety located under the right of the fascia. But although the seating position suited me, a lanky colleague who tried the car said he simply could not fit in. There is only just enough room for the three pedals, and when not in use, the left foot was a bit of a problem to park. I developed a naughty habit of lightly resting it on the clutch—there was nowhere else—but the left leg of a tall person might clash with the pedal and steering wheel.

The essence of the Seven is its performance. The standard Series 4 comes in kit form for £995 with a Ford 1600 GT engine developing 84 bhp. With less than 12 cwt to cart around, that performance is pretty exciting. But for a bit more money you could have a lot more performance. The car which I borrowed at short notice from Caterham Cars' Finchley Road branch had a Holbay Clubman engine pushing out a "guaranteed 120 bhp" at 6200 rpm. It felt like it too! Price in component form is £1,265, slightly more than the twin-cam version (£1,245) and rather less than the Big Valve twin-cam (£1,295). That Big Valver must be the hairiest road-going Seven of all time because the Holbay version had more power than it could sometimes put on the road. The t/c versions apparently have a smoother torque profile.

The Seven is a *sports* car, and considering how much performance you get it is not that much money. It's true that in order to avoid paying tax you have to build it yourself. If the reports that the Government are to introduce new laws in order to obtain that tax are true, then I would recommend any would-be purchaser to buy now. With the dreaded PT it obviously wouldn't be such on attractive buy.

The Holbay is fed through two twin-choke Weber 40 DCOE carburetters, has a hairier R120 camshaft and is fitted with all the best parts that can be mustered. Power reaches the back wheel via a 2000E gearbox with standard ratios, and a 3.7 Escort differential. The clutch on the car I tried was exceptionally stiff, and was very much an in-or-out job; the rear wheels began to bite immediately the critical point was reached.

Operating the clutch in London traffic gave me Charles Atlas-style left leg muscles, but I was very impressed with the car's behaviour in the kind of conditions which obviously do not suit it. The engine ran smoothly throughout the worst traffic jams, never coughing or spitting and remaining at a constant, low temperature. It was extremely tractable, and through all conditions returned a creditable 22 mpg.

But town is not the real habitat of the Seven. It's a country car which will rush up to the legal limit in about 9 sec. At 70 mph in top gear the engine was ticking along at just under 4000 rpm with another 2½ to go. It hadn't even reached its maximum torque, which is produced at 4200 rpm.

Neither is it a motorway car. Although it will tank along at very high speeds, reliably too, the wind and the roar are a little unnerving. I found myself travelling along the motorway more slowly than I do in my Fiat saloon, unwilling to live with the noise but happy in the knowledge that if I wanted to I could bound into the distance.

On minor roads, however, it was a pleasure to drive. It was shatteringly quick, which made for safe over-taking. The road holding was good, certainly in excess of my own capabilities. It was possible to slide the back—perhaps practised Seven owners abuse their cars more than I did—but in normal use it never broke away. The brakes were well up to the job but the pedal needed a good deal of pressure for effect.

The other feature which struck me was the steering. It was several months since I had previously driven a Lotus, and I had forgotten just how precise the steering was. It came as a revelation, simply to flick the car around a corner with the smallest of movements of the steering wheel. With 2¾ turns lock to lock, hands in the easy quarter to three position on the wheel, lying in a well padded seat so close to the ground, it had a real racing feel about it.

Driving the Seven, hood down and windblown, the thought crossed my mind that I had discovered something for which man has been searching for centuries. Is the Lotus 7 the answer to ever-lasting youth?

RICHARD FEAST

The Holbay clubman engine produces 120 bhp at 6200 rpm. 44-17-4

Lotus Seven

There's nothing like it!!!

By Christopher Hilton

It was love at first sight. In the very beginning, I loved her for her beautiful body; and, later, for her heart, too . . .

Of course, as my friends keep reminding me, I am a creature of impulse. I bought a house without ever going inside it and now there I was with a Volkswagen 1300 parked outside the showroom and all kinds of exotic machinery around me.

Then I saw her. Curves and soft lines. Smooth and radiant. Well bred. A suggestion of Aix-en-Provence rather than Chorlton-cum-Hardy. She might have been a model.

A salesman was hovering some distance away. I beckoned him over. It was, he said in a discreet whisper, a Lotus. A what? A Lotus Seven. "I suppose we might be able to arrange a test drive," he added.

I told him I didn't want a test drive. I wanted the car.

"But you don't even know if you'll fit in it!" He seemed mildly amazed by my ignorance. "My dear chap, you have to have been created the right size. The seats are not adjustable." He pointed. Oh, I thought, so those black clamps are the seats . . .

I did get in and thanked God and parents that I was, indeed, the right size, and when he had explained that you had to build the thing yourself and it came through the post, as it were, I knew I wanted a Lotus Seven. Odd, I suppose. I never actually drove one until the pieces had been delivered and it was built. I won't ever forget that day.

The first moment with the car in motion, I thought it had gone mad. First the engine gurgled, then gave forth a gutteral roar which reached such a pitch that it seemed to be snarling and spitting at me. My foot was thrown back by the heavy clutch pedal and the thing took off along the road. Every small mark on the road surface sent a shock-wave rippling through the car—and me. Every time I twitched my trembling fingers on the tiny steering wheel, the car twitched too . . . here, there, everywhere.

Only when I had reached a lay-by, switched off (better to do that, because the car might have a mind of its own) and calmed down did I begin to have doubts. A month later they had all been resolved. I knew I had entered a new world of motoring, so far removed from the ordinary saloon-sports car scene that comparisons aren't valid.

I was now living with a sleek yellow glassfibre beast. Odd, too, that the drawbacks which any road test would highlight—draughts (truthfully, a free passage of wind through the car), doors which did not lock, an open well in the back for luggage, a cramped cockpit to sit in—didn't really matter after a while.

I used to give people runs in it. As we went, I could see them noting these drawbacks. It's nice, they'd say politely, but what did you buy it for?

Well, I did resent the draughts at first—but I got used to that. (In Germany once, it snowed inside the car, lovely, thick flakes). At first I worried about the lack of luggage space, but I learned to plan accordingly, and I used to feel too enclosed in the cockpit until I realised that the position in which the seat held you was precisely the position you should have been in anyway to drive the thing.

But I came to treasure the road-holding. Circling a roundabout in Essex to demonstrate this to a friend, he cried out and covered his face with his hands. We were still comfortably circling the roundabout when he removed his hands to verify, correctly, that we were still very much alive.

Once, too, I came upon an Alpine-Renault—the rally car—in the Vosges Mountains in France. Seeing the Seven on his tail, he began to accelerate round the hair-pin bends. What he resented, I'm sure, was not so much that the Seven was capable of staying with him, but that I was just waiting for the first stretch of straight road to overtake. He definitely didn't like seeing me go past.

The performance, which seemed to press your back against the seat, very much as a big aeroplane does when its engines are suddenly given full throttle to take off, was outstanding.

From traffic lights, no car ever pulled away from the Seven. If you fancy your car a bit and find that statement irksome, there's a very simple test. Find a set of traffic lights with a Seven waiting at them, and see what happens to you.

Then one fine day I parked it and went to work. When I came back in the evening it was gone—"borrowed", taken to Bristol and broken up to remove and sell the 1600 GT Ford engine.

My insurance company provided me temporarily with a Morris Marina. I collected it from Victoria Station, and almost crashed it three or four times. The car just did not do what I wanted it to. The steering was hopeless—like trying to control a trawler in a storm somewhere off Iceland. I tried other cars, and tried honestly to adjust to them. They were all the same: big oblong containers meandering vaguely forward.

Six months later, my twin-cam Seven was on the road. Having learned from the first one, this one was refined by stages (no wind, rain, fog or even snow inside) to the point where I even managed to make all the side lamps work at the same time (a noteworthy feat, judging by other Sevens I have seen). And with the engine properly balanced, there was no need to spend each Sunday morning combing under the bonnet for bolts which had shaken loose during the week.

A whole era is coming to an end if, as Lotus say, the Seven goes out of production.* This brutal, forgiving, funny, frightening little vehicle is the only one around which makes no effort whatsoever at compromise and does exactly what any driver with some beef in him will tell you a vehicle should do.

When you get the hood down—a force nine gale plucking at your face and the level road rising like a tide under your chin—you and the car blend into one unit to make beautiful curves round impossible corners. There just isn't anything like it.

I'm sorry, Mr Chapman. They did say that the road-holding of your Lotus Elans was positively outstanding so I went out of my way to drive one. It's not in the same street.

And another thing. "What do you propose I tell my children and grandchildren when they find a set of old photos in the attic of a yellow, sleek rocket and ask what in the name of goodness it was?" I know what I'll tell them, "Son, you don't know what you missed." □

** New Sevens are at present available in kit form from Caterham Car Sales Ltd., Seven House, Town End, Caterham Hill, Surrey and they will continue to sell Sevens in fully-built form after the introduction of VAT in April.*

LOTUS SUPER SEVEN

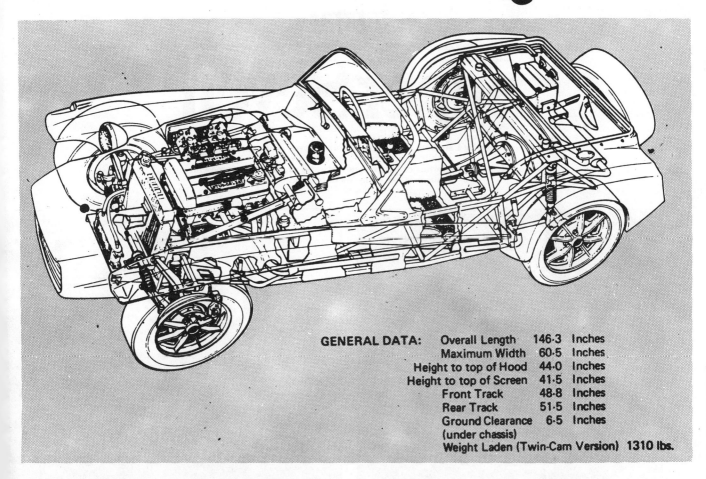

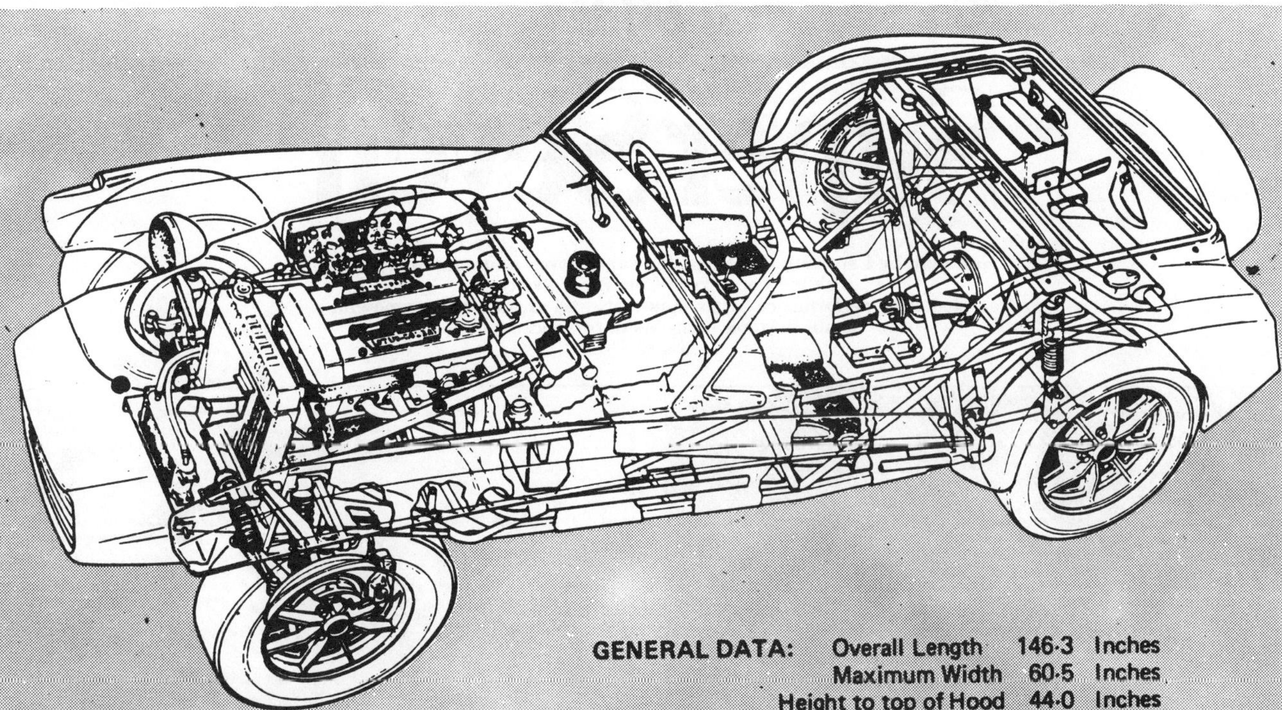

GENERAL DATA:

Overall Length	146·3	Inches
Maximum Width	60·5	Inches
Height to top of Hood	44·0	Inches
Height to top of Screen	41·5	Inches
Front Track	48·8	Inches
Rear Track	51·5	Inches
Ground Clearance (under chassis)	6·5	Inches
Weight Laden (Twin-Cam Version)	1310 lbs.	

LOTUS SUPER SEVEN SAGA

Looking more like a sports car from the vintage era comes the ***Lotus*** *Super Seven. Don't let the externals fool you. Under the bonnet, the twin cam Lotus engine [1558 cc] punch out a 0-50 in 4.9 secs. This puts it among the dragster class. It is an eye stopper that will streak pass the bigger engined and more expensive cars up to 70 mph.*

The power to weight ratio is the answer. The formula was put together by Colin Chapman, designer of the John Player Specials FI racing cars. It that's not fast enough "you can breathe on it a little more and you could chop a few more seconds" says David Nixon export manager for Steel Brothers in New Zealand who hold the franchise for producing these rare species of sports car for a selected market.

There is only one in town and is sitting in Mercantile Motors.

There are no doors to open-just climb and slip in. Once in, the seats "tie" you in, legs can stretch straight out as in a true sports car.

The driving position is a superb straight arm on the leather covered steering wheel. The left arm rests on the central console within easy reach of the well positioned stubby gear stick. Simple and practical is the layout of the instruments. There are as usual Smith tachometer, speedometer and the oil and water gauges similar to the MG layout.

The Umbrella grip handbrake is placed in an akward position under the dashboard on the right hand side of the driver, very difficult to use in an emergency.

Suspension was hard as expected with little or no body roll around bends. Steering was very direct and needed only a short movement to point at the desired direction. Gearshift was like greese-lighting fast, the employment of double declutch gearchanges will bring out the best of the car.

Naturally the last word is accleration. You can feel the G's going through and you seem to run out of road very quickly once you are on fourth. It's so fantastic a gear shift that we will tend to change gears for the hell of changing. Flexible at fourth it pulls very strongly.

Going through the gears we got 40 mph in first second 65 third 85 and top 110.

This is an enthusiasist's car where the price tag should not matter. Around $23,000 a piece. □

Super Seven

Now built by Caterham Car Sales, the Super Seven continues in production with the Lotus Twin Cam Big Valve engine. Shattering performance better than ever. Still as stark and purposeful as the original Lotus Six of two decades ago.

Above: Chris Goffey models the garments which are almost mandatory when driving the Super Seven in wet weather

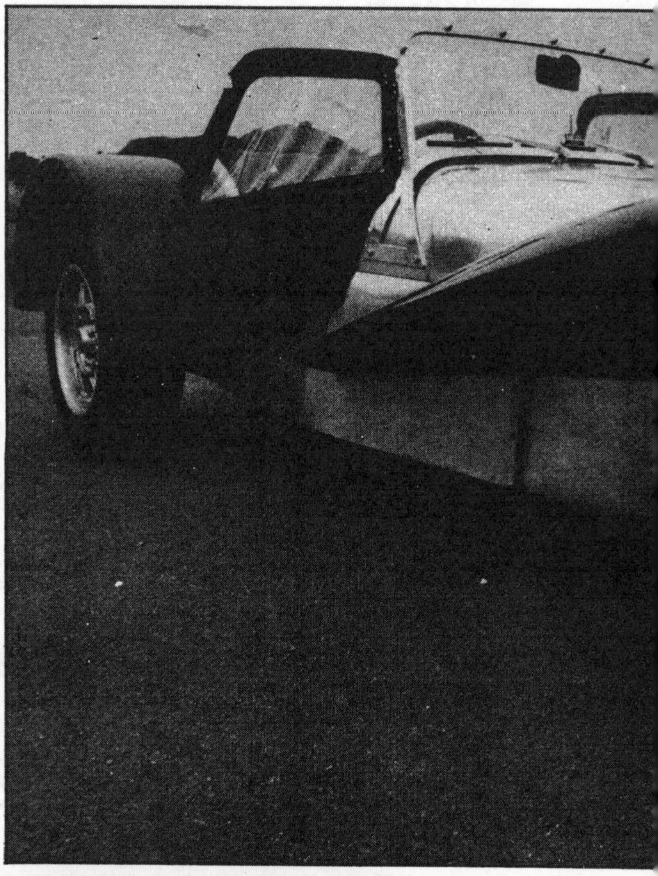

Below: Happiness is an open road, the wind in your hair and a Super Seven

Above: The Series 3 body is much starker and more functional than the more streamlined and now defunct Series 4; there are indicators beneath the headlamps and repeaters on the front wings

Right: The Technical Editor proves that you can squeeze a driver 6ft 2in. tall, weighing 16½ stone into the tiny cockpit

NOBODY WANTED the Lotus Seven to die, least of all Caterham Car Sales who had for some years been the main distributors of the kit versions. So when Lotus announced the cessation of the Series 4 version, Caterham decided to keep the car alive. They bought from Lotus everything that remained – jigs, body-moulds, chassis and spares, in fact, all that was left of the car that started Colin Chapman on the road to success.

It was not difficult for Caterham to decide to revert to building the Series 3 model, since this was the one most loved by enthusiasts. Mike Warner's Series 4 Seven had not been the commercial success that £30,000 of development money tried to make it; and while nobody would deny that it was more practical than earlier versions, it was not what the market wanted. Caterham Cars decided that since the Super Seven should represent ultimate performance, they might as well use the most powerful suitable engine – the Big Valve version of the Twin Cam engine. With its power output of over 120 bhp, this engine could not fail to give the 10·3cwt car blistering performance, which was exactly what we found on re-acquainting ourselves with it.

Performance

Only a handful, and a tiny handful at that, of cars can match the performance of the Super Seven in accelerating from rest to 100 mph in 22sec, and none that we have ever tested reach 30 mph in only 2·3sec. It is simplicity itself to attain such figures since dropping the clutch sharply at 3,000 rpm produces enough wheel spin to enable a delicately-played throttle to keep the engine exactly at maximum torque; when the tyres have stopped spinning, the accelerator can be floored. The change to second gear can be made as quickly as the hand can move just at the moment when the engine revs reach 6,550 rpm, the point at which the rev limiter cuts in. As second is taken and the clutch thumped home another shriek of wheelspin is heard. By now you are doing 40 mph and second gear takes you to just below 60 mph when again the diminutive gear lever can be slashed across the gearbox and

Above: The spare wheel is strapped onto a "space frame" carrier, which also holds the number plate; the body is aluminium, the wings black glass fibre

Below: The spartan cockpit, with fixed seats, tiny steering wheel and neatly Dymo-taped signs for the switches

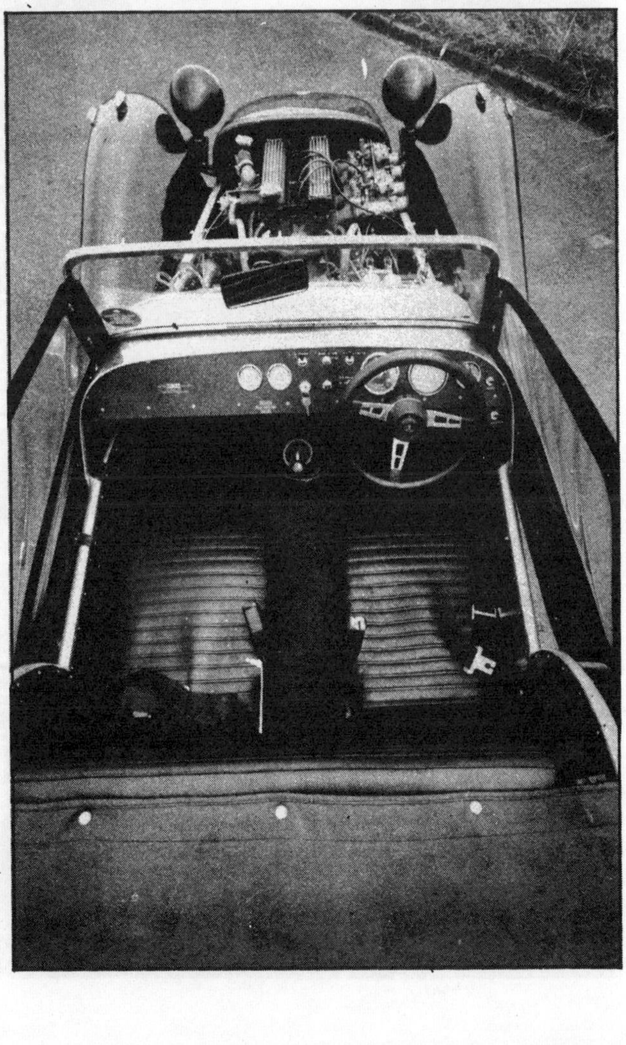

TEST EXTRA

Above: A pair of big Webers lurk behind the right hand headlamp, their gobbling intakes totally unprotected

Left: Seven times Seven: Less agile drivers have to reflect on how to get into the car when the hood is up

Below: The Super Seven is leaned into a right-hander, perfectly under control, although the ride leaves a good deal to be desired

yet *another* cheep of wheelspin is heard as the little car leaps forward in third gear. This is held until 80 mph comes up before the change to top gear is made. You have not yet passed the ¼-mile mark and there is another ¾ of a mile of straight to cover. The ¼-mile and 90 mph come up together and then the affect of the poor aerodynamic shape begins to tell. Another 7sec are needed to reach 100 mph, which is passed only 22sec after leaving the start line. On a slightly windy day for testing 110 mph was reached in only one direction, yet with only a light tail-wind this was achieved in 23·5sec.

No less impressive is the acceleration in each gear, especially in third in which only the 20 mph increment from 50 to 70 mph occupies more than 4sec. In top gear, you get a chance to listen to the changes in engine note as the combination of load and rpm change. Snapping open the throttle at 20 mph produces that hollow gulping sound so typical of unsilenced single side draught chokes for each cylinder. As the revs rise to 3,000 rpm, the exhaust note becomes suddenly hard and gruff. As the revs continue to rise, it goes quieter at 3,500 rpm, and then suddenly hard and very purposeful at 4,000 rpm. After this it just gets more and more shrill as it climbs to its limited maximum of 6,500 rpm, an engine speed reached from 20 mph in just a fraction over half a minute.

Since we used the full performance as often as possible, it was still a pleasant surprise to find that the overall fuel consumption worked out at 23·8 mpg; this can be regarded as a typical figure that an enthusiastic owner might attain. For interest, we took steady-speed fuel consumption figures which showed that at a steady 80 mph, the consumption was still 24 mpg. The DIN consumption figure is 23·4 mpg, which means the 8gal fuel tank gives a range of barely 200 miles.

Roadholding, ride and handling

The roadholding is marvellous, the ride is diabolical and the handling is on the nervous side of reassuring. With so little weight, good grip from the Goodyear G800 tyres and race-proved suspension, one should expect the roadholding to be good. Light steering with plenty of feel tells you exactly what is happening and allows instant correction of the result of any careless or excessive use of the right foot. Basically the Super Seven understeers unless you use power to balance the car, which it is possible to do with only a little practice. The ride is very hard and harsh, even though Caterham have wisely avoided the temptation to use tyres of wider section than is necessary. There is little tendency for either the front or the back of the car to hop over a mid-cornering bump and one would only criticize the tyres for the amount of bump-thump which they transmit.

Despite an overall height of only 3ft, the Super Seven is affected by sidewinds and a sensitive hand must be kept on the steering wheel when passing fast-moving lorries. In still air there is a tendency for camber changes or undulations to cause some self-steering, but it is self-correcting provided that the steering wheel is not held too tightly.

Confrontation: scant attention is paid to aerodynamics, and the negative camber of the front wheels makes the car look almost aggressive

Comfort and controls

The producer of an out-and-out sports car is fortunately relieved of the responsibility for providing too many creature comforts in his cars. Caterham take their lack of responsibility rather seriously, avoiding comfortable seating and any spare room inside the cockpit. They do, however, provide full instrumentation, a tiny thick leather-rimmed steering wheel and the gear lever with about the shortest, sharpest movements on record. The pedals too are designed to be used quickly and often, and on the basis that your foot is rarely off the clutch pedal, they provide nowhere to rest it. However, the combination of brake and accelerator is ideally placed to allow heel-and-toe movements provided that you leave your Cuban-heeled shoes at home.

Bearing in mind the likely use of the car on High Days and Holidays, a heater is a listed option which, in the recent weather we have enjoyed, was unnecessary. Since the heater matrix retains any hot water that is in it, whether or not the water valve is switched off, it is wise to put the water valve in the off position whenever the car is left for any period to avoid the likelihood of unquenchable heat adding to that which comes from the engine and gearbox anyway.

Unlike earlier Lotus Sevens, the Super Seven uses proper headlamps which give good spread and beam, both dipped and main, but side and headlamps must be switched on for daytime flashing. The tiny windscreen boasts washing as well as single speed wiping but the tiny windscreen wipers lift off the screen badly over 80 mph.

Space and stowage

Only the diminutive space behind the fixed and thinly padded seats can be used to stow anything, including the hood when it is in the down position. Thus luggage needs to be of the squashable variety and there cannot be much of it.

Although the position of the seats, pedals and steering wheel are all fixed there is, in fact, adequate room for drivers or passengers of average build up to six feet in height but you need to be very athletic to climb in and out when the hood is erected; our largest staff member (6ft 2in. and currently 16½ stone) was unable to do so at all. With the side screens in place, visibility to the side is severely limited by the inadequate depth of the Perspex panels and with the hood up as well, visibility is limited to the rear, especially when the rear panel gets wet in rainy weather. The rear quarter panels are useful for three-quarter rear vision.

In conclusion

Since September 1974, Caterham Car Sales have managed to maintain a very full book of domestic and world-wide orders for this intriguing little car, to the satisfaction of lovers of fast driving whose budget is limited. You will not see many Super Sevens on the roads of Britain because nearly 95 per cent are exported (mainly to Japan, Germany and Northern Europe). Luckily for us, sales abroad enable Caterham to offer the Super Seven here for less than a Ford Capri 1600GT which, when you consider the performance available, can surely be considered good value for money.

When they took over the manufacture of the car from Lotus, Caterham Cars gave the construction of the chassis to Arch Motors, well-known for their racing car work. Fuller triangulation of the side members was specified to reinforce the radius arm pick-up points, and in addition the engine bay is triangulated at the bottom and the front bulkhead is strengthened by two additional tubes. The steering rack mounting points have now been connected and a steel-tube integral gearbox mounting reinforces the tunnel and floor area. The result of all this work is that the current car feels sturdier and by stiffening the chassis the handling has definitely been improved.

For those who might wish to use an alternative power unit the car can be supplied as a rolling chassis less engine and gearbox for the extremely attractive price of £1,300 (inc VAT) thus avoiding car tax at the same rate as a completed car. The level of this tax is then determined by the purchaser's local Customs and Excise official dependent on the value of the engine and gearbox fitted.

Anyone looking for the creature comforts of today's family car would, of course, be terribly disappointed by the Super Seven, but then a Seven owner would be more than disappointed by the family car's lack of performance. This is a car for the enthusiast, for the man whose car has to feel like an extension of his own will and personality, the extrovert, the competitor. Caterham Cars admit that few owners do long journeys and most use the cars for those occasions when only real performance will send the blood coursing through the veins and bring a sparkle back into their eyes – we loved it. □

Maximum speeds

Gear	mph	kph	rpm
Top (mean)	114	184	6,550
(best)	114	184	6,550
3rd	81	130	6,550
2nd	57	92	6,550
1st	38	61	6,550

Acceleration

True mph	Time secs	Speedo mph	Steady mpg
30	**2·3**	30	
40	**3·2**	42	
50	**4·5**	53	
60	**6·2**	64	
70	**8·3**	75	
80	**10·9**	87	
90	**15·0**	98	
100	**22·0**	110	—
110	—	122	—

Standing ¼-mile: 14·9sec 88 mph
Standing kilometre: 28·2sec 108 mph

mph	Top (1·0)	3rd (1·4)	2nd (2·01)
10–30	—	4·0	3·0
20–40	6·0	3·7	2·6
30–50	5·9	3·6	2·3
40–60	6·4	3·8	—
50–70	6·5	4·3	—
60–80	6·7	—	—
70–90	7·9	—	—
80–100	11·0	—	—

Consumption

Overall mpg: .28·3 (11·9 litres/100km)

Specification

Engine: 4-cyl 82·6×72·8mm (3·25×2·86in.), 1588 c.c. (95·2 cu. in.); CR 10·3 to 1; Dellorto 40 DCOE carbs, 126 bhp (DIN) at 6,500 rpm; max torque 113 lb ft. at 5,500 rpm.

Transmission: Front engine, rear drive. Manual gearbox, ratios, top 1·0, third 1·40, second 2·01, first 2·97, rev 3·32. Top gear mph/1,000 rpm 17·4. Final drive, 3·89 to 1.

Suspension: Ifs, unequal length wishbones, coil springs, telescopic dampers, anti-roll bar. Rear, Live axle, A-bracket, trailing arms, coil springs, telescopic dampers. Steering, rack and pinion, 2·7 turns lock-to-lock.

Brakes: 9in. front discs, 8·0×1·5in. rear drums.

Dimensions: Wheelbase, 7ft 5in. (206cm); front track 4ft 1in. (124cm), rear track 4ft 4in. (132cm). Overall length, 11ft 1in. (336cm), width 5ft 1in. (155cm), height 3ft 1in. (94cm). Turning circle 29ft 6in. (9m). Unladen weight 1,162lb (527kg).

Others: Tyres Goodyear 165HR×13in.; 5½in. rims; Fuel 8 gallons (36 litres).

MANUFACTURER:

Caterham Car Sales, 36–40 Town End, Caterham Hill, Surrey

PRICES	
Basic	£1,690.00
Special Car Tax	£142.83
VAT	£146.63
Total (in GB)	**£1,979.46**

Extras	
*Goodyear alloy wheels	£68.58
*Seat belts	£16.74
*Stainless steel exhaust	£24.30
Full tonneau cover	£20.20
*Oil cooler	£24.84
*Heater	£27.00
Aeroscreen	£10.26
*Adjustable dampers	£21.60

**Fitted to Test Car*

THE SUPER SEVEN LIVES!

If eating a lotus makes a person dreamy and forgetful of home and friends, what will driving one do?

BY DOUG NYE

PHOTOS BY GEOFFREY GODDARD

TWO TRADITIONAL BRITISH sports cars have always had an attraction bordering on the addictive. One, the Morgan, has thrived for years and looks like soldiering on forever. The other, the Lotus Seven, was almost killed off by its parents but luckily found a good foster home. It is still alive and well in the town of Caterham, south of London.

Caterham Cars Ltd (Seven House Town End, Caterham, Surrey, England) has lived with the spartan little Lotus for 17 years, ever since they became Lotus' first agents in 1959 when Colin Chapman stopped selling Sevens direct from the Cheshunt works. In 1968 Graham Nearn, Caterham Cars' Managing Director, arranged a sole concession to take all the Seven kit cars that Lotus could build. Then Lotus Components decided to take the model up market and meet growing export legislation. In April 1970 they replaced the classic old S3 aluminum box and its race-bred performance with a kind of trod-upon Tupperware beach buggy known as the Seven Series 4. The new model was more roomy, more civilized and more legislation-complying than the deposed S3 but lacked much of the old hair-shirt character. It was a kind of "squeezed out of a tube" car and Lotus sank some £30,000 into development to break into the MGB/TR6 market: It failed dismally.

When Lotus moved even further up market the basic Seven theme became just too *infra dig* to survive. Nearn and Caterham Co-Director David Wakefield knew there was still a demand to be supplied and they acquired total manufacturing rights for the Seven, including all the jigs, body molds, components and spares.

They set up Seven Cars Ltd in a corner of their modest Caterham works and began production with the S4 only to confirm their suspicions that it wasn't quite what the Seven customer wanted. The decision to ax the unloved and unlovely S4 and resurrect the aluminum-paneled S3 virtually made itself. Ultimate performance was to be the idea and with the Big Valve version of the 1558-cc Lotus-Ford twin-cam engine, the tiny 1162-lb Super Seven really fills the bill. Its 126 bhp gives it a power-to-weight ratio reminiscent of the downfield runners in the 1961 Grand Prix season! It is virtually identical to a strong Formula Junior or cooking Formula 2 for 1963–1964 and as a road car that makes it exciting enough to be real fun.

Seven Cars produced their first S3 Twin Cam in September 1974, and that car has spent some happy months in Hong Kong and is about to accompany its owner on a move to Hawaii. After an initial rush of home orders as the good news spread, 90 to 95 percent of the Sevens were supplied to export customers. Today home demand is growing, but export orders still take up most of Caterham's productions.

Component supply has always been a problem in maintaining a steady flow of Sevens and while Nearn and Wakefield would like to build four or five a week they are currently averaging less. A current dearth of engines from Lotus clouds the immediate future, but still the demand appears insatiable and Seven Cars is in the happy position of not wanting too much publicity in case they can't keep pace.

The Seven is available in knocked down and completed form, the kit including a virtually assembled rolling chassis. Its body/chassis unit is complete with wiring, instruments, wiper motor, weather equipment and holes drilled for wing fittings. The engine and gearbox are complete and placed in the chassis with the driveshaft, while the suspension is loosely fitted to ease loading onto a trailer. David Wakefield reckons almost anyone could have the car running on a Sunday evening after taking delivery on Friday and just to assure the worried customer his → 6

The Lotus Seven frame of mind

Top: The Lotus Seven in its element — hillclimbing. Above: Patrick Depailler started racing in 1964 in this Lotus Seven

By Eoin S. Young

PATRICK DEPAILLER was exhausted but supremely contented, tired more by the barrage of interviews he had been giving non-stop since he won the Monaco Grand Prix in his Elf-Tyrrell. "Now," he said with a smile, "Now, I can afford to buy my car!" Patrick could, of course, buy just about any car he cares to fancy, but the boyish little French driver tends to share his fascination of money with the Scots — he loves making it quite a lot more than he loves spending it . . . .

The car Patrick wants to buy is a twin-cam Lotus Seven as a reminder of those weekends in 1964 when he raced a car for the first time. It was a stripped Seven, and looking back on it, he loved it. Lotus Sevens are not really cars in the ordinary sense of the word, they are more a frame of mind, a habit you find yourself falling into.

The latest Series 3 Super Seven from Caterham Cars in Surrey would comfortably beat the performance of Depailler's racing Seven. In road-going form with the Lotus 1600cc twin-cam engine, the Super Seven is close to being the fastest accelerating production car to sixty miles an hour, a speed that arrives in a hectic fraction over six seconds. It doesn't accelerate, so much as explode off the line. Top speed is fairly academic in a car like this because you tend to use the rivetting performance through the gears, arriving at your cruising speed just short of the total discomfort barrier — 70 mph is a woffling 4,000 rpm. For the record, *Autocar* tested maximum velocity on the Super Seven at 114 mph. The Lotus Seven grew from Colin Chapman's earliest sporting interest in Austin Seven specials and the Seven today embodies all the elements of those early cars — electrifying performance from a lightweight car, swift steering, wind in the hair, minimal weather equipment, that essential element of discomfort so that you *know* you must be enjoying it, a Vintage theme with modern mechanicals.

When Colin Chapman took his Lotus group of companies upmarket with the Elites, Elans and finally the Esprits and Eclats, he had to make the decision to leave the spartan Seven behind. Lotus had tried to civilize the Seven with the Mark IV version but it rather fell between two stools — it was *not* a car with the same Vintage spirit as the Series 3, it was more modern and glass fibre. When Lotus decided to bury the Seven, small specialist companies stepped in to take over. Graham Nearn, managing director of Caterham Cars at Caterham in Surrey, had built up a strong business selling and servicing Sevens, so he arranged to take over the rights and equipment to manufacture the Series 3 Seven. David Dixon, marketing manager for Steel Brothers half a world away in New Zealand, saw the Lotus Seven as a relatively simple addition to the assembly of lorries and heavy earth-moving equipment, so he picked up the later-model Series IV Seven to serve the Colonies. Yet another Seven arrangement was made with a Spanish company to build the Series IV using Fiat running gear.

The fact that Colin Chapman and his Lotus company had decided to move away from the Seven concept didn't mean the concept was dying — simply that Lotus had outgrown it. The market was very definitely still there as Caterham Cars and Steel Brothers were able to show.

The evolution of the Seven has been barely perceptible since leaving Lotus, apart from those modifications required by modern regulations governing safety in the construction of motor vehicles. The other major balk in the path of Seven progress was that the customer didn't want it any other way than the way it was. Doors and wind-up windows would have been the beginning of the end for the man who wanted a Seven because it was still the way Colin Chapman had designed it 20 years ago. It isn't that those original Lotus Seven customers out-grew the car over two decades because Seven enthusiasts grow like carrots — every year there is a new crop of young enthusiasts with bobble hats and scarves. Graham Nearn doesn't categorise his customers into age groups, saying simply that his customers are "car enthusiasts, mainly." If there is any determining factor to age it is insurance, and for this reason Nearn says the money-up buyers tend to be 22 and older. There is no doubt that Nearn could increase his production to more than 150 cars a year and cut the six-month wait for delivery, but it makes more sense to preserve the almost cottage-industry aspect of Seven-building along with the six-month security of a full order-book.

As the supply of Lotus 1,600 c.c. twin-cam engines began to dry up, Nearn negotiated a supply of engines based on the 1,600 c.c. Ford engine with an actual capacity of 1,598 c.c., instead of the previous engine based on the old 1,500 c.c. Ford unit bored out to 1,558 c.c. Power output on the earlier engine was 126 bhp (DIN) at 6,500 rpm with a compression ratio of 9.5 to 1, whereas the new engine with an extra 40 c.c. maintains the horsepower figure while running with a compression ratio of 8.5 to 1 on 4-star petrol instead of 5-star premium petrol which is becoming more difficult to find in Britain.

The hood of the Lotus Seven is one of the less lovely things in the world of motorcars and getting in or getting out with the top up requires a very special knack. It is a car meant for top-down motoring, a high days and holidays car for use preferably when the sun is shining. At the wheel of the Seven, your eyes are a mere 3ft from the road and you sight down a louvered bonnet between the headlights. It doesn't take a very determined flight of fancy to imagine the lights are P100s and the long louvered bonnet is that of an SS 100 Jaguar . . . . Except, of course, that the Seven is a great deal faster than the SS100 was. It really is a four-wheeled version of a Superbike with many of the attendant stimulations for the arteries.

Right: Twin cam Lotus engine as installed in the Mk 3 Caterham-built Lotus Seven

Below: The Mk 3 Seven combines vintage qualities with modern mechanicals. You get the same "wind in the hair" fun from £3,000 worth of Lotus Seven as you do from £13,000 worth of vintage Bentley

The Steel Brothers Series IV Seven in New Zealand is on the verge of a major revision within the parameters of the traditional styling. The changes have been demanded by the need to maintain a reasonable volume of production by investigating markets beyond the rather restrictive confines of New Zealand. "In 1977 we put together the idea of fitting the 2-litre Elite motor and five-speed gearbox into an extended and developed Series IV, so that we could offer a car suiting the pollution and safety requirements of the more developed markets in either right- or left-hand drive," says David Dixon. "Our initial prototypes have proved that the new 16-valve engine and five-speed gearbox marriage to the Seven is practical and successful and results in a smoother, faster car with adequate appeal for the international sports car market. Our next step is to improve the cockpit by fitting a new modular dashboard layout to suit left- or right-hand drive, increasing the cockpit room and improving the weatherproofing. We hope this will extend the car beyond the market of the enthusiast only."

The new 2-litre car will be officially known as a Lotus 907. The engine bay has been increased by three inches in length and four inches in width and the engine itself is canted over at an angle of 45 degrees. The new Lotus engine/transmission package is 50lb heavier than the old. Overall length has been increased by eight inches. The cockpit comes in for major attention and will be four inches wider and three inches longer to allow more elbow room as well as adjustable seats. Dixon plans to have New Zealand wool carpets and leather upholstery. New sidescreens have been designed which incorporate proper handles and locks. The fuel tank has been increased from 7.5 gallons to 8 gallons. Early test figures show the 2-litre 907 capable of a standing quarter mile in 14.5sec with a top speed quoted at around 130 mph although this may be easier to attain on paper with a gear ratio chart than it is on the open road.

Use of the Elite engine means Steel Brothers can offer their car with "domestic" or "Federal" versions where export markets require them. Thus the 907 for the New Zealand market will be fitted with the 160 bhp version of the engine, and the Americans will have the anti-pollution 130 bhp version.

Top: The hood is not one of the car's more attractive features

Above: 2-litre engine cants at 45 degrees in New Zealand Lotus 907. Engine bay is 4 in. wider, 3 in. longer

Prototype Lotus 907 at Ruapuna race circuit near Chistchurch beside a 500c.c. Cooper-Norton. Bikes in background: 500 Manx Norton, 750TZ Yamaha

Following completion of Dixon's development programme on the 907, overtures have already been made to the obvious overseas export markets. It is not beyond the bounds of possibility that the New Zealand-built car will be imported to Britain for sale in the Panther Lima segment of the sports car market.

I drove an early prototype — one was already in the States, another in Australia for local evaluation — and as a Lotus Seven it was transformed. The engine develops 160 bhp at 6,200 rpm and the extra urge, compared with the Caterham Seven, comes through in a much more refined manner. The Caterham car is unashamedly a front-engined Formula Atlantic car in a moderate state of tune for public consumption. Motoring hard in the Caterham car brings with it the all-round sound of hard motoring. The blast of air through the carburettor intakes almost drowns the rorty exhaust note and over everything you have the roar of the wind in the rigging. This sonic dimension is one of the extras that customers are delighted to pay for with a Caterham Seven, but out in New Zealand the Seven is being de-noised. The car has become smoother and more civilised to extend it, as Dixon says, beyond the market of the pure enthusiast. Both Dixon and Nearn may be right in their separate ways of pursuing customers since their markets now seem unlikely to clash.

The market which caters for wind-in-the-hair enthusiasts may be an invigorating one but it has to be inevitably low volume and this was the main reason why Lotus cut the Seven adrift. Colin Chapman, the man behind the automotive perfection of the latest Lotus 79 Grand Prix car and a string of trend-setters and winners before it, was also the designer of the Seven and he has never really abandoned his thoughts for a "fun car." He still talks wistfully about building a "Son of Seven" one day when the pressure is off, but you get the distinct impression that pressure, with A. C. B. Chapman, is never off or even turned down a little. He is a man with a total commitment to success; second place, to Chapman, is losing. He thinks a successor to the Seven might be a three-wheeler, a modern Moggie trike. It would have no refinements like doors, just step-over cutaways for elbows because it would be a "elbows-out" sort of motorcar. As with the original Morgans, Chapman thought the best form of power unit would be a motorcycle engine — perhaps one of the latest four-cylinder Superbike motors with close to 100 bhp, or a more traditional large-capacity vee-twin slogger like a Harley Davidson. Two wheels at the front, one at the rear.

The way Colin Chapman discussed the little car that exists only in the back of a busy mind, you have the distinct impression that it might not mirror the success of the Esprit and the Eclat on the showroom floors of dealers around the world, but wouldn't it be fun?

Chances are that Chapman will never get around to the spare moments he needs to commit his "fun car" to paper, so the present Lotus Seven in its traditional Series 3 form in Britain or in its revitalized 907 form in New Zealand will remain as the ultimate for the enthusiast who wants to get the feel of what sports cars were all about. □

Caterham Cars,
Seven House, Town End, Caterham Hill, Surrey CR3 5UG, England.
Steel Brothers (NZ) Ltd,
PO Box 11-077 Sockburn, Christchurch 4, New Zealand.

For those who want to put honest fun back into driving, the Seven means . . .

A SPORTING CHANCE

Sports cars come and sports go, but the Seven just keeps on keepin' on. An immortal design. Eoin Young explains about England's traditional version and New Zealand's exciting Lotus 907.

The sports car . . . *Lotus Seven style.*

PATRICK DEPAILLER was exhausted but supremely contented, tired more by the barrage of interviews he had been giving non-stop since he won the Monaco Grand Prix in his Elf-Tyrrell. "Now," he said with a smile, "now, I can afford to buy my car!"

Patrick could, of course, buy just about any car he cares to fancy, but the boyish little French driver tends to share his fascination of money with the Scots — he loves making it quite a lot more than he loves spending it . . .

The car Patrick had in mind was the twin-cam Super Seven as a reminder of those weekends in 1964 when he began racing. It was a stripped Seven, and looking back on it, he loved it. Super Sevens are not really cars in the ordinary sense of the word, they are more a frame of mind, a habit you find yourself slipping into.

The latest Series 3 Super Seven roadster from Caterham Cars — no longer called a Lotus — in Surrey would comfortably beat the performance of Depailler's racing Seven. In road-going form with the Lotus 1600 twin-cam engine, the Super Seven is close to being the fastest accelerating production car to 95 km/h, a speed that arrives in a hectic fraction over six seconds. It doesn't accelerate, so much as explode off the line.

Top speed is fairly academic in a car like this because you tend to use the riveting performance through the gears, arriving at your cruising speed just short of the total discomfort barrier. 110 km/h is a woofling 4000 rpm. For the record, "Autocar" tested maximum velocity on the Super Seven at 183.4 km/h.

The Lotus Seven grew from Colin Chapman's earliest sporting interest in Austin Seven specials and the Seven today embodies all the elements of those early cars — electrifying performance from a lightweight car, swift steering, wind in the hair, minimal weather equipment, that essential element of discomfort so that you *know* you must be enjoying it, a vintage theme with modern mechanicals.

A prototype Lotus 907 (the NZ-made development of the Series IV Seven) amid some fine machinery including Cooper Norton Formula III car, Manx Norton and Yamaha TZ750 bikes, and Lotus Esprit.

When Chapman took his Lotus group of companies upmarket with the Elites, Elans and finally the Esprits and Eclats, he had to make the decision to leave the spartan Seven behind. He had tried to civilise the Seven with the Mark IV version but it rather fell between two stools — it was *not* a car with the same vintage spirit as the Series 3, it was more modern and glassfibre. When Lotus decided to bury the Seven, small specialist companies stepped in to take over.

Graham Nearn, Managing Director of Caterham Cars at Caterham in Surrey, had built up a strong business selling and servicing Sevens, so he arranged to take over the rights and equipment to manufacture the Series 3 Seven.

David Dixon, marketing manager for Steel Brothers half a world away in New Zealand, saw the Lotus Seven as a relatively simple addition to the firm's assembly of lorries and heavy earthmoving equipment, so he picked up the later-model Series IV Seven to serve the colonies.

Yet another Seven arrangement was made with a Spanish company to build the Series IV using Fiat running gear.

The fact that Colin Chapman and his Lotus company had decided to move away from the Seven concept didn't mean the concept was dying — simply that Lotus had outgrown it. The market was very definitely still there as Caterham Cars and Steel Brothers were able to show.

The evolution of the Seven has been barely perceptible since leaving Lotus, apart from modifications required by modern regulations governing car safety. The other major balk in the path of Seven progress was that the customers didn't want it to change. Not at all. Doors and wind-up windows would have been the beginning of the end for the enthusiast who wanted a Seven because it was still the way Colin Chapman had designed it 20 years ago.

It isn't that those original Lotus Seven customers outgrew the car over two decades because Seven enthusiasts grow like carrots — every year there is a new crop of young enthusiasts with bobble hats and scarves. Graham Nearn doesn't categorise his customers into age groups, saying simply that his customers are "car enthusiasts, mainly".

If there's any determining factor to age it is the high cost of insurance. That's the reason, Nearn says, that the money-up buyers tend to be 22 and older. There's no doubt that Nearn could increase his production to more than 150 cars a year and cut the six-month wait for delivery, but it makes more sense to preserve the almost cottage-industry aspect of Seven-building along with the six-month security of a full order-book.

As the supply of Lotus 1600 twin-cam engines began to dry up, Nearn has negotiated a supply of engines based on the 1600 Ford with an actual capacity of 1598 cm^3, instead of the previous engine based on the old 1500 Ford bored out to 1558 cm^3. Power output on the earlier engine was 93.8 kW at 6500 rpm, running 9.5:1 compression ratio. The new engine maintains that power, using 8.5:1 compression ratio.

The Super Seven's soft-top is one of the less lovely things in the world of motorcars, and getting in or getting out with the top up requires a very special knack. It is a car meant for top-down motoring, a high days and holidays car for use preferably when the sun is shining. At the wheel of the Seven, your eyes are a mere metre from the road and you sight down a louvred bonnet between the headlights. It doesn't take a very determined flight of fancy to imagine the lights are P100s and the long louvred bonnet is that of an SS100 Jaguar . . . Except, of course, that the Seven is a great deal faster than the SS100 was. It really is a four-wheeled version of a Superbike with many of the attendant stimulations for the arteries.

The Steel Brothers Series IV Seven in New Zealand is on the verge of a major revision within the parameters of the traditional styling. The changes have been demanded by the need to maintain a reasonable volume of production by investigating markets beyond the rather restrictive confines of New Zealand.

"In 1977 we put together the idea of fitting the two-litre Elite motor and five-speed gearbox into an extended and developed Series IV, so that we could offer a car suiting the pollution and safety requirements of the more developed markets in either right- or left-hand drive," says David Dixon. "Our initial prototypes have proved that the new 16-valve engine and five-speed gearbox marriage to the Seven is practical and successful. It results in a smoother, faster car with adequate appeal for the international sports car market. Our next step is to improve the cockpit by fitting a new modular dashboard layout to suit left- or right-hand drive, increasing the cockpit room and improving the weatherproofing. We hope this will extend the car beyond the market of the enthusiast only."

The new car will be officially known as a Lotus 907. The engine bay has been increased by 75 mm in length and 100 mm in width and the engine is canted over at 45 degrees. The new Lotus engine/transmission package is 20 kg heavier than the old. Overall length has been increased by 200 mm. The cockpit comes in for major attention and will be 100 mm wider and 75 mm longer to allow more elbow room as well as adjustable seats.

Early days. 1953 saw the first production Lotus . . . the Mark 6. It was replaced in '57 by the first Seven.

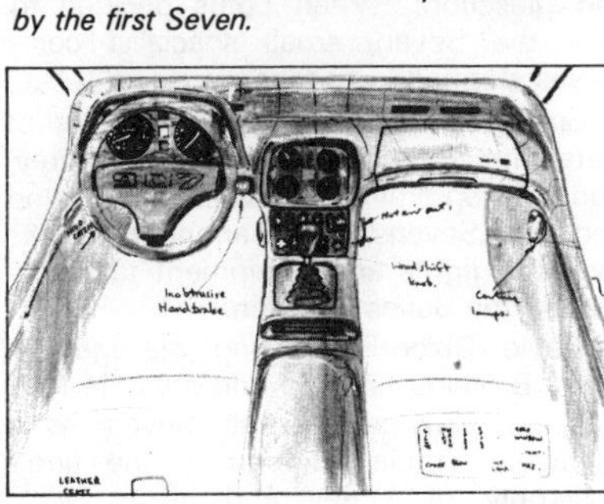

Artist's impression of the dash layout for Steel Brothers' Lotus 907. The modular instrument panel facilitates left- and right-hand drive versions. Cockpit has wool carpet and leather upholstery.

Dixon plans to have New Zealand wool carpets and leather upholstery. New sidescreens have been designed which incorporate proper handles and locks. The fuel tank has been increased from 34 litres to 36. Early test figures show the two-litre 907 capable of a standing quarter mile in 14.5sec, with top speed quoted at around 210 km/h although this may be easier to attain on paper (with a gear ratio chart) than on the open road.

Use of the Elite engine means Steel Brothers can offer their car with "domestic" or "Federal" versions where export markets require them. Thus the 907 for the New Zealand market will be fitted with the 120 kW version of the engine, and the Americans will have the anti-pollution 97 kW edition.

Dixon says overtures have already been made to the obvious overseas export markets. It is not beyond the bounds of possibility that the New Zealand-built car will be sold in Britain, in the Panther Lima segment of the sports car market.

I drove an early prototype — one was already in the US, another in Australia for local evaluation — and as a Lotus Seven it was transformed. The extra urge, compared with the Caterham Seven, comes through in a much more refined manner.

The Caterham car is unashamedly a front-engined Formula Atlantic car in a moderate state of tune for public consumption. Hard driving in the Caterham car brings with it the all-round sound of hard motoring. The blast of air through the carburettor intakes almost drowns the rorty exhaust note and over everything you have the roar of the wind in the rigging. This sonic dimension is one of the extras that customers are delighted to pay for with a Caterham Seven, but out in New Zealand the Seven is being denoised.

Both Dixon and Nearn may be right in their separate ways of pursuing customers since their markets now seem unlikely to clash. Catering to wind-in-the-hair enthusiasts may be invigorating but it also means low volume and that was the main reason why Lotus cut the Seven adrift.

Colin Chapman has never really abandoned his thoughts for a *fun car*. He still talks wistfully about building a "Son of Seven" one day when the pressure is off,

That the Seven doesn't lend itself to cosmetic refinements is shown by this 1963 add-on kit with curved windscreen, fibreglass hardtop and gull-wing doors.

Above: Caterham Cars builds about 150 of the Series 3 version annually.

Left: In the new Lotus 907 the two-litre Elite engine is canted at 45 degrees to reduce bonnet height. Engine bay (and cockpit) width and length are increased.

but you get the distinct impression that pressure, with A.C.B. Chapman, is never off or even turned down a little. He is a man with a total commitment to success; second place, to him, is losing.

Chapman thinks a successor to the Seven might be a three-wheeler, a modern Moggie trike. It would have no refinements like doors, just step-over cutaways for elbows because it would be an "elbows-out" sort of motorcar. As with the original Morgans, Chapman thought the best form of power unit would be a motorcycle engine — perhaps one of the latest four-cylinder Superbike motors worth close to 75 kW, or a more traditional large-capacity Vee-twin slogger like a Harley Davidson. Two wheels at the front, one at the rear.

The way Colin Chapman discussed the little car that exists only in the back of a busy mind, you have the distinct impression that it might not mirror the success of the Esprit and the Eclat on the showroom floors of dealers around the world, but wouldn't it be fun?

Chances are that Chapman will never get around to the spare moments he needs to commit his fun car to paper, so the Lotus Seven in its traditional Series 3 form in Britain, or in its revitalised 907 form in New Zealand, will remain as ideals for enthusiasts who want to get the feel of what sports cars were all about. □

CONTINUED FROM PAGE 60

company offers a complete post-build inspection. Delivery currently takes five or six months but the basic kit could be simplified to save some time.

Although the Lotus Seven spirit has been retained, Caterham has not been afraid to make some improvements. Space frames have extra diagonals to limit flex and there is a new mounting for the Triumph Herald steering rack. The battery has been relocated to prevent the bonnet shorting it out and such legislative devices as a collapsible steering column and steering locks are now available. Optional extras include a heater, air horns, full tonneau cover and adjustable dampers all around.

Basically the Super Seven, as the Caterham car is known, is pure Lotus, with independent coil and wishbone front suspension and a Ford Escort live rear axle sprung on coils and controlled by an A-frame and trailing arms. Wheels and tires are by Goodyear, 13 x 5½Js shod with 165-13 G800 radials.

The Super Seven is a very narrow car, made to just barely accommodate two slim people. I'm far from slim and 6 ft tall, so when Wakefield eased me into the driver's seat we looked around for a tire lever to get me out again. I felt like the man who fell into Rob Walker's cider press. My knees hadn't been so friendly for years. I could feel nothing but anonymous pedals beneath my shoe leather and there was only one thing to do—remove my shoes. I stored them on the comfy passenger seat and my piggies could then differentiate 'twixt clutch, brake and throttle, and find a resting place beneath them. The thick-rimmed steering wheel sat perfectly at arm's length and the tiny gear lever snuggled into my palm. Good instrumentation includes a fuel gauge, ammeter, tachometer redlining at 6500 rpm, an optimistic 130-mph speedometer and combined oil pressure/water temperature dial. A bank of olde English toggle switches surround the ignition lock in the dash center.

So David hinged in the sidescreen and fastened it with turnbuckle and pop-stud while explaining about "our burst-proof door locks." Out on the road my initial impression of the Seven is of an abiding flatness and lowness, just the colored wings flaring into view on either side of its polished aluminum bonnet and those vintage headlamps up front to sight along. And it flies.

From a standstill it's simple to drag away with spinning wheels and the engine pulling hard from around 3000 rpm. The Elan Sprint gearbox has the shortest lever I've ever seen and you just blink to snatch 2nd, blink again for 3rd then top with the tires chirping with wheelspin in each intermediate cog! Sitting with the back axle fighting away just behind one's lumbar region, there's a lot of car up front, which was embarrassing in tightly twisting lanes and at junctions where visibility was poor. Ninety-degree corners find the wavy sidescreens an embarrassment too, for you want to see through them, cannot and attempt the Super Seven neck-stretch as you try to peer over them.

Roadholding is incredible. There's a deal of self-steering over ripples but the Seven runs true if you hold the wheel loosely and slinging through curves and corners is just a matter of lifting one fist or the other an inch or two. With very little practice the Seven can be slammed around at will, flicking into smooth fishtails out of tighter turns but always willing to come back and scurrying cross country at astonishing average speeds.

The disc/drum brakes are smooth and powerful but the car is so light that an over-enthusiastic downshift can lock the rear wheels momentarily, which makes things sound more exciting than is seemly. Ride? Well, yes, you can ride in it . . . one can hardly say more, but ride quality isn't the point. This little car is fun—so much fun you just can't believe it's still allowed.

During our day with the Seven we had only two nasty moments. One was when some horsemen appeared ahead, right arms extended, wanting to turn across the road. I slowed and waved them over, then snicked into 2nd and the tractable little Seven burbled round behind them. Just then I glimpsed the last horse's towering rump, fully 4 ft above my head—and its tail was lifting! Thank the Lord for quick cars. The tires smoked and we escaped, but it did demonstrate a potentially pungent problem with such a low roadster.

Then while Geoff was taking some stationary pictures I turned to say something and found the rear mudguard exactly at kneecap reflex height. Can't say I recommend that either.

But for the enthusiastic motorist the Super Seven with its super car potential is a back-to-nature experience not to be missed. It's crude, it's uncompromising, but it's also sheer, unadulterated, unbelievable fun.

With superb roadholding, quick steering and immense acceleration, the Super Seven is the ultimate fun

CATERHAM SUPER SEVEN

A ball of fire

As all motoring enthusiasts know, the famous Lotus Super Seven was taken over by Caterham Car Sales, who produce a much improved version. Now fitted with the big-valve twin-cam engine, this little ball of fire packs 126bhp into a machine weighing 11cwt, and that ain't hay.

First of all, let's get one thing straight. I'm tired of reading that the Super Seven is not a practical, everyday car. When I was a lad, I used sporting vehicles, such as the chain-driven Frazer-Nash and the 30/98 Vauxhall, as my sole means of transport. These splendid vehicles had none of the luxury of the Super Seven, which has sidescreens and even a heater, while their gearlevers and hand-brakes were outside in the cold. Yet, I thought it perfectly normal to attend social functions in white tie and tails and would certainly do the same in the car from Caterham, though dinner jackets are more usual in this less formal age.

The design follows that of the earlier Seven and the later, more plasticky variation has been forgotten. The improvements are unseen, but they make an enormous difference. The chassis is still a space-frame with a stressed aluminium skin, but it is far more rigid, thanks to additional triangulation. The location of the rear axle has received a great deal of attention and the beam itself has been stiffened by a full-length, welded-on web. This has also overcome the old problem of the bolts moving and letting out the oil. The front suspension is still that of the original Formula 2 Lotus single-seater.

The improvement in ride and roadholding is almost beyond belief. This is particularly noticeable in the form of vastly better traction, the hopping of the rear axle having been eliminated, which is also advantageous on bumpy corners. The ride is not nearly as hard as I expected and on most road surfaces one travels in quite reasonable comfort.

After all these years, the twin-cam engine has become outstandingly reliable and, although it produces a lot of power from 1558cc, it develops massive torque in the middle ranges and has good low-speed flexibility. Praise must be given to the two twin-choke Dellorto carburettors, which give instant starting and immediate throttle response.

While the exhaust note at high revs is inspiring, it makes rather a flat sound at low speeds and might attract unwelcome attention — I would prefer to have a more absorbent silencer. The open carburettor chokes are not too noisy for this sort of car, but pancake filters would keep road dirt out of the engine — they are available.

Vintage shape

With so much power and so little weight, the Super Seven can see off any of the £25,000 exotica in initial acceleration and the easy gearchange, with a very narrow gate, assists this sparkling performance. The car reaches 90mph extremely quickly, but thereafter the vintage shape takes its toll. The headlamps, wings, and screen create an enormous aerodynamic drag, and although acceleration continues past 100mph, this is reflected in the far greater power needed to propel the machine. Very economical of fuel below 90mph, the Super Seven becomes thirsty at higher speeds.

I remember testing a TT Replica Frazer-Nash which would not lap at more than 80mph round the Brooklands outer circuit. Upon removing the lamps, front wings, and screen, it immediately achieved more than 100mph, with a best lap at 103mph. It is understandable, therefore, that the Super Seven is not at its best at very high speeds, but does this matter? Speed limits are tending to restrict continuous fast driving and perhaps many people will be content to call it a day at 112mph or so. To drape the car with aerodynamic bodywork would destroy much of its unique appeal, and the additional weight would make it less of a Lamborghini-eater from a standing start.

The driving position is excellent and all the controls are well placed, though there is no free space for the left foot. A well-built driver might find himself wedged in the Super Seven, but a spot of amateur panel-beating would soon produce some extra bum-room. I feel that the sidescreens are a bit too vintage, for their wide edges and rippled panels make driving in London an awkward business; perhaps something a little more rigid could be devised. The hood causes entering and leaving the vehicle to become a gymnastic feat, but it should not be beyond the wit of man to devise something better. This is an open car and one would not use the hood for real driving, but it's useful to be able to erect it for town work.

Marvellous fun

The whole point of the Super Seven is that it's marvellous fun to drive. There's nothing difficult about it and almost anyone would enjoy it, but only a competent *conducteur* can make it display its full magic. In the hands of a real coachman, there is practically nothing on wheels that can look at it on a winding road. This combination of roadholding, quick steering, and immense acceleration adds up to about the safest car that's made anywhere. When you flick past a mimser who is wandering all over the road, you are past him and gone before he has time to hoot his pathetic little horn in his fury.

There is no need for fine weather in order to enjoy the Super Seven. With the hood down, I roared through rain, hail, and even a little snow without getting wet, and the powerful heater kept my feet and legs warm. The petrol tank is on the small side and the luggage space is far from generous, but the Super Seven is so enjoyable to drive that one forgives it for a few imperfections.

When I road tested its predecessor, the Lotus Mark 6, the price of the kit was £425. However, that was with a side-valve 1172cc Ford engine and a three-speed gearbox. The price of the Super Seven may seem steep for so compact a vehicle, but to find another car that will accelerate from a standstill to 60mph in 6secs you will have to pay many times its price.

Unfortunately, you must be prepared to wait nine months for delivery and, for idiotic legal reasons, you must do the last bit of the assembly yourself, even though the total price now includes tax and VAT. Such things may frighten away the dilettante, but the real enthusiast will be willing to spend some time and trouble to get his hands on this little gem of a car. Although I suppose I am old enough to have reached years of discretion, I reckon that the Super Seven is the ultimate for fun on wheels. ■

Specification and performance data

The hood is always down for real *driving.*

Car Tested: Caterham Super Seven open sports 2-seater, price £4464. Extra: seat belts £19.87, heater kit £41.58, light alloy 6in wheels and Goodyear Grand Prix tyres £102.60, rollover bar £26.46, air horns kit £12.91.

Engine: Four cylinders 82.55x72.75mm (1558cc). Compression ratio 10.3 to 1. 126bhp DIN at 6500rpm. Twin chain-driven overhead camshafts. Two twin-choke Dellorto carburettors.

Transmission: Single dry plate clutch. 4-speed synchromesh gearbox, ratios 1.0, 1.40, 2.01, and 2.97 to 1. Hypoid rear axle, ratio 3.54 to 1.

Chassis: Tubular space frame with stressed aluminium panels, glassfibre wings and nosecone. Independent front suspension by wishbones, coil spring damper units and anti-roll bar. Rack and pinion steering. Live rear axle on trailing arms, central A member, and coil spring damper units. Disc/drum dual-circuit brakes. Bolt on light-alloy wheels, fitted 185/70 HR 13 tyres (extra).

Equipment: 12-volt lighting and starting. Speedometer. Rev counter. Oil pressure, water temperature, and fuel gauges. Heater. Windscreen wipers and washers. Flashing direction indicators.

Dimensions: Wheelbase 7ft 5in. Track 4ft 1in/4ft 4in. Overall length 11ft 1in. Width 5ft 1in. Weight 11cwt.

Performance: Maximum speed 112mph. Speeds in gears, third 88mph, second 62mph, first 42mph. Standing quarter-mile 14.5s. Acceleration: 0-30mph 2.2s, 0-50mph 4.5s, 0-60mph 6.0s, 0-80mph 10.8s.

Fuel Consumption: 22 to 28mpg.

The lusty, 126bhp, big-valve, twin-cam engine.

The 1982 Caterham Super Seven

BROOKLANDS BOOKS

LOTUS SEVEN—ELAN

LOTUS ELAN 1962-1973
The Elan 1500, 1600, Coupé, S2, 2+2, SE, S4, Sprint, +2S, 130S, 2S130 and S 130/5 are reported on. Some 8 Road Tests, a track test, a road research report and comparison test Vs the TR6 are included.
100 Large Pages

LOTUS ELAN COLLECTION No. 1
This collection of articles covers the whole production life of the Elan from 1962 to 1974 and supplements the Elan marque book with completely different articles. Six Road Tests are included together with an owner survey a 24,000 mile report, and advice on buying a used Europa. Models covered include the 1500, 1600, S/E, Plus 2, Sprint, 2S130, and the S3.
70 Large Pages

LOTUS SEVEN 1957-1980
A total of 28 articles tell the Lotus 7 Story from its introduction in 1957. They are made up of 11 Road Tests, an owners report, comparison tests plus stories on racing and history. Models include the America, 7, Super 7, Cosworth, Twin-Cam, IV, Seven Mazda, Caterham 7 & Twin-Cam.
100 Large Pages

LOTUS SEVEN COLLECTION No. 1 (1957-1982)
The views of Britain, Australia, Malaysia and the U.S.A. are expressed in the 26 articles that trace the Lotus Seven story from its inception in 1958 to the Jubilee Model introduced to celebrate the model's 25th Anniversary. Articles cover 8 road tests, a touring trial, racing, history, assembly and new model introduction. Cars covered are the Seven, Super Seven, 1500, Series 4, 4SE, S4, plus the Caterham Super Sevens.
70 Large Pages

These soft-bound volumes in the 'Brooklands Books' series consist of reprints of original road test reports and other articles that appeared in leading motoring journals during the periods concerned. Fully illustrated with photographs and cut-away drawings, the articles contain road impressions, performance figures, specifications, etc. None of the articles appears in more than one book. Sources include Autocar, Autosport, Car, Car & Driver, Cars & Car Conversions, Motor, Motor Racing, Modern Motor, Road Test, Road & Track and Wheels. Fascinating to read, the books are also invaluable as sources of historical reference and as practical aids to enthusiasts who wish to restore their cars to original condition.

From specialist booksellers or, in case of difficulty, direct from the distributors:
BROOKLANDS BOOK DISTRIBUTION, 'HOLMERISE', SEVEN HILLS ROAD, COBHAM, SURREY KT11 1ES, ENGLAND. Telephone: Cobham (09326) 5051
MOTORBOOKS INTERNATIONAL, OSCEOLA, WISCONSIN 54020, USA.
Telephone: 715 294 3345 & 800 826 6600